WHAT PEOPLE ARE
You Were Made to FLOURISH

Jesus told us that He came to give us not just life, but abundant life. *You Were Made to Flourish* will encourage you to lean into Jesus and take hold of all of God's promises for your life so that you can live the abundant, fruitful, purpose-filled life you were created for.

Christine Caine
Best-selling author, Founder of A21 and Propel Women

I can tell you, I've known Sarah Wehrli for . . . GOSH, almost twenty years, and she's one of the most caring people I've known, in my lifetime! She has a special gift that recognizes the BEST in people and then, draws it out of them. If you feel STUCK and want to totally transform your life, you have to start from the inside-out. You Were Made to Flourish. . . . and my friend, Sarah, can show you how!

Nicole Crank
Host of the *Nicole Crank Show*, author, speaker,
Co-Pastor of FaithChurch.com

You were created on purpose for a purpose with dreams and goals God's counting on you to fulfill. In *You Were Made to Flourish*, Sarah guides you, with practical keys and biblical wisdom, to break free from barriers holding you back and step into a thriving, abundant life.

Terri Savelle Foy
Founder of Terri Savelle Foy Ministries, author,
speaker, cheerleader of dreams

Ever feel like you're just getting by? Then this book is for you! Each page is full of uplifting wisdom and achievable action steps that will help you move from surviving to thriving in every area and season of life. You won't want to put it down!

Alli Worthington
Business coach and author of *Remaining You While Raising Them*

Sarah is a phenomenal wife, mom, friend, and leader. Her heart to serve and see people come to know Jesus is inspiring! I know there are so many people on the other side of this incredible devotional who will be encouraged and empowered to move forward and become all that God has called them to be.

Oneka Mcclellan
Co-Pastor of Shoreline City Church Dallas

You were made to flourish! It's something we all desperately want to believe, but we struggle when we don't know how. Sarah makes the way clear and inviting in this practical, inspiring devotional guide. If you're looking for life-change, this is your book!

Beth Jones
Founding Pastor, Valley Family Church, author, *Reinvent: Start Fresh and Love Life*, and the *Getting a Grip on the Basics* series, TV Host, *The Basics With Beth*

We live in a day where a gospel of self-empowerment is preached and positive mantras are proclaimed all in hopes of attaining a full life. While the desire to live a flourishing life is what our Heavenly Father desires for us to have, oftentimes in pursuit of such a life we end up with the wrong guidance. What I appreciate about Sarah, having known her for many years is that she does know how to flourish! She understands that it can only be accomplished in the pursuit of knowing Jesus intimately. On these pages you will find no fluff, rather you will discover principles that you can put into practice and receive the fruit of His abundance in your life.

Colleen Rouse
Author and Founding Pastor of Victory Atlanta Church

Fruitfulness is every heart's goal, but it can discourage us when the process takes time. In this compelling read, Sarah offers fresh insight on how to build a life that flourishes in season after season. Put these truths into action, and your life will never be the same!

Anne Christiansen, Pastor of Jesus Church Oslo
and Co-Founder of Jesus Revolution

Published by Four Rivers Media

For foreign and subsidiary rights, contact the author.

Cover design by: Sara Young
Cover photo by: Rachelle Celeste Photography

ISBN: 978-1-959095-04-0   1 2 3 4 5 6 7 8 9 10

Printed in the United States of America

10 KEYS TO
THRIVING IN
EVERY SEASON

You were made to FLOURISH

SARAH WEHRLI

CONTENTS

*The righteous will **flourish** like a palm tree,*
they will grow like a cedar of Lebanon;
planted in the house of the LORD,
*they will **flourish** in the courts of our God.*

–Psalm 92:12-13

THE PROMISE OF FLOURISHING: AN INTRODUCTION

Whoever trusts in his riches will fall, but the righteous will flourish like a green leaf. —Proverbs 11:28 (ESV)

When my family and I lived in Orlando, I developed a love for palm trees. We had one in our front yard, and I would often look out my window and admire its beauty. It was as if I grew more peaceful and joyful just watching its leaves blowing effortlessly in the summer wind. Perhaps that's why I love Psalm 92:12-15 (AMP) so much—because it compares you and I to a palm tree. The passage says:

> *The righteous will flourish like the date palm [long-lived, upright and useful]; They will grow like a cedar in Lebanon [majestic and stable]. Planted in the house of the Lord, They will flourish in the courts of our God. [Growing in grace] they will still thrive and bear fruit and prosper in old age; They will flourish and be vital and fresh [rich in trust and love and contentment]; [They are living memorials] to declare that the Lord is upright and faithful [to His promises]; He is my rock, and there is no unrighteousness in Him.*

11

There's one word that stands out to me in this passage: *flourish*. Here's how Webster's Dictionary defines it: "To grow luxuriantly; to increase and enlarge, as a healthy, growing plant; to be prosperous."[1] Some of its synonyms include: "thrive, prosper, expand, multiply, spring up, shoot up, bloom, blossom, bear fruit, and burst forth."[2] In *every* season, the palm tree flourishes, and Jesus promises that we can, too! We can prosper in our health, relationships, careers, and finances. We don't have to settle for simply surviving from day to day; We can *thrive* and enjoy the life we've been blessed with!

I can't wait to unpack the spiritual keys that help us do so. Before we begin, though, there are a few things I want you to know. First, I want you to feel how genuinely excited I am for you and for the opportunity for life change you are about to encounter. The truths in these pages can bring incredible progress if you'll let them! Second, I want to encourage you to find a person or possibly a small group to walk with you through this process. They can either work through this study with you, or they can help keep you accountable as you do. Whomever you choose, make sure you trust them to help you pursue God's best, as you put the truths you read into action.

Third, please know that this book is unique in its nature. It is both a devotional and a study guide (what I like to call a devotional guide!), so you'll find several items after each chapter. You'll find questions for reflection which are incredibly important, so don't rush through them! Set aside a generous amount of time to think

---

1 "Webster's Dictionary 1828 - Flourish," Websters Dictionary 1828 (American Dictionary of the English Language), accessed January 23, 2023, https://webstersdictionary1828.com/Dictionary/flourish.
2 Conny Stewart, "Flourish," The Whole Living Hub, April 22, 2020, https://thewholelivinghub.com/flourish/.

through your answers and record your thoughts in the journal space provided.

You'll also find a passage for further study. These passages will help build your faith and perspective on the keys highlighted in each chapter. I recommend using a study Bible for this part, taking notes from it in the journal space provided. Then, you'll find a call to action. This is to ensure your progress. As you take the steps provided, you'll begin moving from surviving to thriving, strengthening your roots to outlast any storm. Next, you'll find a prayer to help you start a conversation with God about the key presented in the chapter.

Finally, at the end of each chapter, you'll find a short story of flourishing. These testimonies come from people who have experienced the truth of what you're learning. Read these stories with confident hope, knowing that God is no respecter of persons. What He has done for them, He *will* do for you!

I can't wait to dive into these chapters with you. Are you ready? Grab your coffee or tea, your Bible, and a pen, and let's get started.

Chapter One

CONNECT TO THE SOURCE

I am the way, and the truth, and the life. No one comes to the Father except through me. —John 14:6 (ESV)

When my older kids were young, I took them to an organic farm. This farm was full of various beautiful fruits and vegetables, but Isaac and Lizzy were most excited about the strawberries. They were in awe as they plucked the big, bright, beautiful berries off the vines one by one and put them in their baskets.

A few minutes of *oohing* and *ahhing* later, one of them asked, "Mom! How do these strawberries stay so fresh? There's no refrigerator!" I couldn't help but laugh. Typical city kids! They didn't know better, so I held up a vine and explained. "Because they are connected to *this*, they receive water and nutrients regularly," I said. "When we pluck them off, they die, but when we leave them connected to the source, they flourish!"

The kids nodded, then continued picking strawberries, but I kept contemplating that reality. With each pluck of the berries, I thought about how true this same concept is to all of our lives. We live refreshed and continuously flourishing when we connect to our Source—*Jesus*—the Vine of Life.

Connect

In John 15:1-8 (MSG), Jesus explained this to His disciples. The passage says:

> *I am the Real Vine and my Father is the Farmer. He cuts off every branch of me that doesn't bear grapes. And every branch that is grape-bearing he prunes back so it will bear even more. You are already pruned back by the message I have spoken. Live in me. Make your home in me just as I do in you. In the same way that a branch can't bear grapes by itself but only by being joined to the vine, you can't bear fruit unless you are joined with me. I am the Vine, you are the branches. When you're joined with me and I with you, the relation intimate and organic, the harvest is sure to be abundant. Separated, you can't produce a thing. Anyone who separates from me is deadwood, gathered up and thrown on the bonfire. But if you make yourselves at home with me and my words are at home in you, you can be sure that whatever you ask will be listened to and acted upon. This is how my Father shows who he is—when you produce grapes, when you mature as my disciples.*

Friends, God *wants* us to be fruitful. That's why He gave us Jesus! But we won't flourish because we have the *opportunity* to connect to Him. We have to actually *do* it! When we connect to the Vine, we gain what we need to flourish in every area of our lives, in every season of our lives.

One of my favorite parts of this passage is that it shows Jesus' love for us clearly. We see that He isn't content with us simply bearing fruit. His heart is that we bear *much* fruit. He doesn't just want us to *survive*; He wants us to *thrive*. Ephesians 3:20 says that God wants "to do immeasurably more than all we ask or imagine." His heart longs to take us from glory to glory, strength to strength, and faith to faith.

It's important to realize that this fruit is not just referring to religious activities; it's referring to us actually becoming more like Jesus. The more we connect to Him and spend time with Him, the more like Him we become. And the more like Him we become, the more we invite blessing into our lives. Galatians 5:22 tells us that as we remain connected to Jesus, we naturally reap the fruit of His Spirit in our lives—fruit like love, joy, peace, longsuffering, kindness, goodness, faithfulness, gentleness, and self-control. This fruit speaks loudly of God's goodness and faithfulness to those around us, bringing honor and glory to Him.

The key to bearing much of *this* kind of fruit starts with connecting to the Source, but it doesn't end there. We've got to commit to the connection, resolving to abide in Jesus, no matter what.

Commit

I grew up in a Christian home, and my parents were pastors. I accepted Jesus as my Savior at a young age and learned much about

Him throughout my childhood years. However, though I *connected* to Him early in life, I didn't *commit* to Him until I was a freshman in high school.

I was 14 when I first had an encounter with Jesus myself. I remember sitting in a youth camp worship service when He spoke to me.

He asked, "Sarah, am I first in your life?"

I thought, Well, I'm a good person. I mean, I'm saved, and you know I love you, Jesus.

He interrupted my thoughts. "No, Sarah. Am I your *best* friend?"

I looked down the row where my friends were sitting and realized I couldn't honestly answer *yes*. With conviction, I responded, "No, Jesus. You're *not* my best friend. But I want you to be."

This experience caused me to realize that until that point, I had cared more about what my friends thought about me than what Jesus did. It helped me see that I no longer wanted only to *connect* to Him; I wanted to live *committed* to Him. My heart longed to develop a continual relationship with Him, so that night, I committed to our connection.

From that chapel service on, I pursued my relationship with Jesus relentlessly. I learned to recognize His voice, discern His leading, and understand His character. I felt what it meant to truly be His *friend*.

When I did, I began gratefully enjoying flourishing in every area of my life.

As the years have progressed, I've naturally assumed more responsibility—first as a college student and employee, then as a wife and later, as a mom. Throughout each new season, I have had to become more intentional about my commitment. There are days distractions seem to appear from every angle, as the enemy attempts to pull me away from my First Love. There are even times I have given in, veering from the Source, and I can feel it. In those moments, the Lord is faithful to convict me and remind me to press in. When He does, I slow down, identify and remove the distraction, reconnect to the Source, recommit to the connection, and eventually, return to flourishing.

Throughout the years and their seasons, I've discovered that of all the things we can fill our lives with, our relationship with Jesus is undoubtedly the most important. Matthew 6:33 (NLT) says, "Seek the Kingdom of God above all else, and live righteously, and he will give you everything you need." In Him, we find all the joy, peace, wisdom, clarity, and direction we could ever hope for.

Now, I want to ask you: Who is *your* source? Where do you get *your* fulfillment? Is it from a person? A spouse, friend, or family member? Is it from a job, position, or title? Is it from your bank account, status, or social media following? These things are not wrong in themselves, but to continually flourish, there can only be one answer to this question: Jesus. He *alone* must be our Source. He must be our very best friend.

Jeremiah 17:7-8 compares our commitment to Jesus to a tree planted by a stream. It says:

> *But blessed is the one who trusts in the Lord, whose confidence is in him. They will be like a tree planted by the water that sends out its roots by the stream. It does not fear when heat comes; its leaves are always green. It has no worries in a year of drought and never fails to bear fruit.*

No worries and *no* fear—*no matter* what happens around it. The tree planted by water *never* fails to flourish! What an incredible promise! When we too connect to and remain committed to our Source, we can flourish in any environment, circumstance, and season.

In the heat of opposition, attacks, and persecution, we can flourish.

In the wilderness, in the desert, and in the storm, we can flourish.

Even in the midst of a pandemic, a recession, and tumultuous global events, we can flourish.

Because we are connected to the Source of all life, we can bear *much* fruit—*no matter what*!

Shine

It's a beautiful experience to begin seeing the fruit produced from your commitment. When you do, it's easy to think it's all for your benefit; however, that couldn't be further from the truth. Just as the strawberries flourish for those who eat them, and the tree flourishes for those who sit in its shade, we flourish for others, too. We flourish to glorify God and draw people to Him.

The NIV translation it like this in John 15:8: "This is to my Father's glory that you bear much fruit, showing yourselves to be my disciples." Here, Jesus makes it clear: our fruit is for God's glory. We're blessed so that we can be a blessing! It's like a lamp. When the lamp connects to the power source, it shines. But it doesn't shine only for itself. It shines so that everyone around it can benefit from its light!

My deepest hope and prayer is that you live connected to *and* committed to the Source so that your life constantly flourishes. I realize you may not be there just yet, though. Today, you might find yourself in one of two other positions. First, you could be disconnected. You might have heard of Jesus but never started a relationship with Him. If so, I invite you to turn to Appendix A at the back of this book and pray the Salvation prayer. If you'll embrace what it means to walk with Jesus, your life can flourish, becoming more beautiful than you ever thought possible.

Second, you could be connected to Jesus but not committed to Him. Maybe you continually allow distractions to pull you from the Source, finding yourself far from flourishing, yearning for a deeper intimacy with Jesus that you might have once had. Thank God, His mercies are new every morning! You don't have to remain burdened by life's worries, searching for nourishment from inferior sources. You can choose to commit to the one true Source today. If you're ready to commit, I invite you to pray the prayer with me at the end of this chapter.

Once you've connected to and committed to Jesus, I urge you to remain consistent. If you feel yourself veering, stop and identify the distractions. Then, reconnect, recommit, and embrace the beautiful things God brings to pass in your life, as He takes you from glory to glory and grace to grace! Colossians 2:6-7 encourages us in this when it says, "So then, just as you received Christ Jesus as Lord, continue to live your lives in him, rooted and built up in him, strengthened in the faith as you were taught, and overflowing with thankfulness."

When we *connect* to the Source and *commit* to seeking Him daily, our lives *shine* brightly, bringing glory to our Father and testifying of His goodness to those around us. Friend, you *can* bear abundant fruit, even amid famine. You can shine brightly with hope, even amid dark discouragement. You were *made* to flourish!

GOD DOESN'T WANT US SIMPLY TO SURVIVE; HE WANTS US TO THRIVE!

Questions for Reflection:

1) Take time to discover where you stand today. Have you connected to Jesus? Have you acknowledged Him as the Savior of your life? Are you committed to Him? Do you have an ongoing, deepening relationship with Him as your best friend? Write out where you are. Then, write out where you would like to be.

_____

_____

_____

_____

_____

_____

_____

_____

_____

_____

_____

_____

_____

_____

_____

_____

_____

_____

2) Think about what parts of life you gain the most fulfillment from. Which of these sources is not Jesus? How can you take steps today to ensure Jesus remains your Source?

_____

_____

_____

_____

_____

_____

3) Identify a part of your life that is currently flourishing. How can you shine the light of what God has given you with others? If you can't think of an area that is flourishing, think of one you're believing will flourish. What will you share when it does?

_____

_____

_____

_____

_____

_____

Passage for Further Study:
Colossians 1:15-18

Call to Action:

In the journal space provided, put your answer from number three into a statement of promise. First, express your commitment to God. Promise Him that you will spread His light as He causes you to shine. Then, write *how* you will do this. Tell Him practically how you will share His goodness with others when He causes that area of your life to flourish.

_____

_____

_____

_____

_____

_____

_____

_____

_____

_____

_____

_____

_____

_____

_____

_____

_____

Prayer for Today:

Jesus,

I want to know you as my best friend. Please forgive me for seeking fulfillment apart from you. Today, I commit to reconnecting to you, my Source, for the rest of my life. I trust you to fulfill your promise to keep me refreshed and renewed as I stay connected to you.

In Your name I pray,

Amen

Story of Flourishing:

As a pastor's wife and member of our faith community, I have always enjoyed loving and serving people. As the years went on, though, I went beyond loving it and started to pride myself in it. I felt ministry was my identity and thought my work ethic and effort to please produced my worth. This led to exhaustion and deep unhappiness.

It was as if the more I strived, the less I measured up. I was on a hamster wheel of performance that only led to increasing discontent. Finally, the reality hit that I wasn't *thriving* in life and ministry. I was barely *surviving*.

In desperation, I sought God's help. The Holy Spirit showed me I was the problem to the joy I was seeking because I was searching for identity in my own efforts—not God's. It was a process, but as I learned to view *Him* as my Source, I received a renewed love for my Savior and a joy like I had never known. I rested in Christ and what He's already done for me.

My life and ministry began to truly thrive when I made this shift in my heart: Jesus is enough. Because of Him, I am, too.

—Chantelle

Chapter Two
GET A VISION

Where there is no vision, the people perish . . . —Proverbs 29:18 (KJV)

I visited another farm recently and learned a lot about the planting process. As I stood staring at the empty fields, the farmer of that land struck up a conversation with me.

"You can't tell now," he said. "But in the spring, these fields will be full." His eyes lit up as he excitedly named off the various fruits and vegetables he intended to plant and pointed to where they would grow.

The farmer's passion and vision inspired me. It reminded me that just like the planting process, in our lives, vision is vital to flourishing. We must see the fruit on the inside before we will ever see it on the outside. That's because when we clearly see the goal for tomorrow, we can better decide what actions to take today. Because the farmer had a vision for what crops he wanted to harvest, he knew what seeds to plant, and what steps he needed to take to ensure those seeds flourished.

Make it Plain

You might think, *Having a vision sounds great, but where do I get it from? And how do I know if it's God's vision for me, too?* James 1:5 (NKJV) says, "If any of you lacks wisdom, let him ask of God, who gives to all liberally and without reproach, and it will be given to him."

We gain vision by coming to God in prayer, sitting quietly with Him, and listening for the thoughts and ideas He brings to our hearts. When seeking God's vision, I often use Ephesians 1:18-19 as a guide for prayer. It says:

> *I pray that the eyes of your heart may be enlightened in order that you may know the hope to which he has called you, the riches of his glorious inheritance in his holy people, and his incomparably great power for us who believe...*

Here, we find a clear picture of God's promise to open the eyes of our understanding to know Him and His purposes in a greater way.

VISION IS VITAL TO FLOURISHING.

When praying for vision, we should seek it for every area of our lives. God created us as three-part beings. We have a soul (our mind, will, and emotions), a spirit, and a physical body. 3 John 1:2 (NKJV) confirms this when it says, " . . . I pray that you may prosper in all things and be in health, just as your soul prospers." Every part of our lives matters to God. So, we can ask Him with confidence, "How do you want me to prosper in my family life? In my career? In my finances? In my health?"

Just like God wants us to flourish in every area of our lives, He wants us to flourish in every season of our lives, too. Flourishing looks different for each person and in each season. Flourishing in your twenties will look different than flourishing in your forties. Flourishing as a single woman will differ from flourishing as a mother or a grandmother. When we pray for and receive renewed vision for each of life's seasons, we can take actions to ensure we reap an abundant harvest in each one.

WE MOVE TOWARD WHAT WE FOCUS ON. THE MORE WE SEE OUR VISION, THE MORE WE WILL PURSUE IT.

Once you feel you have gained a solid picture of God's vision for every area of your life, as well as for your unique season, take the next practical step. Make it plain by writing it down. Habakkuk 2:2 (NKJV) says, "Write the vision and make it plain on tablets, That he may run who reads it."

When you have the vision clearly written, place it somewhere you will see it often. I put mine on a vision board in my office. This board is full of images, scriptures, and goals for the year. It serves as my daily (sometimes, hourly!) reminder to continue moving forward. Keeping the vision before us is crucial to progress because we always move toward what we focus on. The more we see our vision, the more we will naturally pursue and move toward it.

Prepare the Ground

The next thing the farmer talked about was the part of the process he was currently in—the part that comes after gaining vision. He was preparing the ground to plant.

"Right now, it looks ugly because I'm in the preparation stage," he explained. "It might not seem like it, but this stage is vital to the process. I'm moving debris out of the way, so when I plant the seed, it will grow properly."

This is our next step, too. After we gain vision from God and make that vision plain and present, our next steps will become clear. Thoughts, attitudes, and habits contrary to our vision will become obvious, and we'll have to prepare the ground of our hearts to become good soil for the seeds we will plant. We might discover we need to do away with clutter, distractions, and hindrances. We might find we need to deal with fear, complacency, or past disappointments. Whatever it is, we must clear the ground and prepare the soil for the seed to grow to its full potential.

Walk by Faith

After that enlightening conversation with the farmer, I continued my trek around the farm. I looked at the barren ground and thought, *He's right–this does look ugly! I wonder how he is so confident this land will produce a harvest.* The truth is: the farmer's confidence didn't come from knowing anything; it came by faith in the power of a seed.

We, too, must walk by faith in order to flourish. Even in dry preparation seasons, we must believe our harvest will come. We've got to trust the vision God has given us, and hold on to the promise, reminding ourselves constantly of His faithfulness. Our God is the same yesterday, today, and forever. He has fulfilled promises since the beginning of time, and He continues to do so today!

When my older two kids were young, Caleb and I planned a family beach trip for the end of the year. Two weeks before we were to leave, we told them about it. Immediately after the conversation, Isaac and Lizzy ran to their rooms, put on their swimsuits, got their towels, and started "laying out" in the living room.

I laughed and said, "Guys, we have two weeks until we are leaving!"

Lizzy replied, "I know, Mom! I'm just imagining I'm already there. I'm preparing myself!"

I often think back to this story when I'm waiting on a promise from God. My kids had so much faith that our words were true. They believed they were going to the beach, so they acted like they were already there. *That* is the kind of faith we must embrace to flourish in season after season. Even in the preparation stage, when our fields look desolate, we've got to see our harvest in faith and live like it's on the way.

EVEN WHEN OUR FIELDS LOOK DESOLATE, WE'VE GOT TO SEE OUR HARVEST IN FAITH AND LIVE LIKE IT'S ON THE WAY.

Walking by faith is never easy, but the result is worth it. If we will keep planting and persevering, our lives *will* flourish! And this flourishing is not just for us; it is a vital part of God fulfilling His vision on the earth.

One of my favorite quotes comes from the esteemed late evangelist Myles Munroe. He said:

> *The wealthiest place in the world is not the gold mines of South America or the oil fields of Iraq or Iran. They are not the diamond mines of South Africa or the banks of the world. The wealthiest place on the planet is just down the road. It is the cemetery. There lie buried companies that were never started, inventions that were never made, bestselling books that were*

never written, and masterpieces that were never painted. In the cemetery is buried the greatest treasure of untapped potential.[3]

THERE IS AN INVALUABLE TREASURE IN YOU, AND IT NEEDS TO COME OUT!

I believe this is what the Lord is speaking to you today: There is an invaluable treasure in you, and it needs to come out! So, set aside time to tune out distractions and tune in to the Lord. Ask Him to give you a vision and write that vision down. Then take steps—prepare the soil of your heart, clearing the debris, and plan to plant the seeds that will bring a beautiful harvest. Finally, walk in full faith, confident you will reap the harvest. If God has spoken it, you *will* see it!

---

3 "A Quote by Myles Munroe," Goodreads, accessed January 23, 2023, https://www.goodreads.com/ quotes/9196732-the-wealthiest-place-in-the-world-is-not-the-gold#:~:text=%E2%80%9CThe%20 wealthiest%20place%20in%20the%20world%20is%20not%20the%20gold,It%20is%20the%20 cemetery.

Questions for Reflection:

1) What would it look like for you to flourish in your life? What would it look like to flourish in your relationships and in your career? In your health and in your finances? Write your answers in the space provided.

_____

_____

_____

_____

_____

_____

_____

_____

2) Is there something blocking your soil from bearing fruit? Maybe it's clutter, distractions, or bad habits. What about fear, complacency, or past disappointments? Write as many as you can think of. Then, commit them to the Lord, asking Him for wisdom and grace to prepare your heart-soil for fruitfulness.

_____

_____

_____

_____

_____

_____

3) What doubts do you have about the dreams God has given you? Write them out. Then, search your Bible for a promise of God that counteracts every fear. Anytime you doubt, speak that verse out loud, declaring that you will see God's vision come to pass in every area of your life.

_____

_____

_____

_____

_____

_____

_____

_____

_____

IF GOD HAS SPOKEN IT, YOU WILL SEE IT!

Passage for Further Study:

Jeremiah 29:11-13

Call to Action:

Set aside time to tune out distractions and seek the Lord for vision. Even if you feel you already have vision for every area of your life, ask God to confirm and fine tune it. Then, write that vision down. Next to it, write three steps you can take toward those dreams this year, and add due dates. Finally, create notifications in your phone calendar, or write them in your planner. However you do it, make sure you take those steps toward making the vision a reality.

If you ever begin to doubt in the process, return to your page with God's promises, speaking them out loud, as many times as you need to. For further help discovering your purpose for this season, I encourage you to check out my book *Awake: Rise to Your Divine Assignment,* where I discuss this topic in more depth.

_____

_____

_____

_____

_____

_____

Prayer for Today:

Lord,

Open my eyes to see, my heart to receive, and my mind to understand the great purpose you have for me. Please make clear your vision for my life, in every area: in my spirit, in my soul, and in my body. Give me clarity regarding your plan for my relationships, my career, my health, my ministry, and my finances. Open my eyes to new possibilities as you guide me to identify and remove any hindrances. Then, help me to walk by faith as I keep my eyes and heart set on your promises.

In Jesus' name,

Amen

Story of Flourishing:

I was raised by a single mom. We lived in shelters and used food stamps to get by. I hated the suffering my family endured, and I hated seeing other people suffer, too. I knew at a young age I wanted to help people stop the suffering in their lives.

After high school, I played basketball for a college in Oklahoma. While there, I got a young girl on campus pregnant, threw away my basketball opportunity, and incurred over four hundred thousand dollars in debt. It was there I felt I had hit rock bottom. I was suicidal, just trying to make it each day for my new child.

It was this most painful time in my life that helped to clarify my purpose. I began to renew my mind with God's word, and it was then I received a vision from God about how to bring help and healing to others through my life. For the last seventeen years, I have been blessed to train others to win in every area of life. I have trained entrepreneurs, pro athletes, and CEOs. I have built seventeen championship teams as the youngest Director of Performance in the nation at the Division 1 level and have worked with athletes from the NBA, NFL, MLB, and MLS, as well as with Olympic athletes.

Today, our nonprofit serves over four thousand first responders and military personnel from over one hundred seventy-eight different agencies. I have started five businesses, authored six books, have an apparel brand and a supplement line, and am blessed to speak in a variety of settings. I am grateful for all that I endured because it helped me find vision. My mess truly became my message, and my greatest test became my greatest testimony!

—Jonathan

Chapter Three

BELIEVE IN THE SEED

*The grass withers and the flowers fall, but the word
of our God endures forever. —Isaiah 40:8*

I learned so much on my trip to the farm. Perhaps the most life-changing takeaway I gained, though, was an accurate picture of the seed's power. Though tiny, it holds unbelievable potential inside, waiting to be released. But to release it, the farmer must first recognize this potential, despite it seeming insignificant.

In Matthew 13, God's Word is compared to a seed. Just like a farmer, to release the Word's potential in our lives, we must live aware of its power. When we do, we will revere it. We will prioritize preparing our hearts to receive it. Then we will consistently plant it, protect it, and nurture it. We will intentionally set aside daily time to study Scripture, meditate on God's truths, and stand on His promises in prayer.

Eating Well

Throughout Scripture, we not only find God's Word compared to seeds but also to sustenance. Matthew 5:6 (AMP) says:

> *Blessed [joyful, nourished by God's goodness] are those who hunger and thirst for righteousness [those who actively seek right standing with God], for they will be [completely] satisfied!*

In Hebrews 5:12, we read that a spiritually mature believer needs "strong meat," and Jesus calls Himself the Bread of Life (John 6:35) and the Living Water (John 4:10). It makes the truth abundantly clear: God's Word is fuel for our spirit and nourishment for our souls! When we partake of it consistently, like healthy food, it keeps us energized and alert.

As a wife and mom with an usually packed schedule, I'm often faced with the choice between healthy, nourishing food, and unhealthy fast food. While fast food is okay sometimes, I know that if my family and I consistently try to gain our nourishment from it, we'll find ourselves sluggish and eventually, unhealthy.

This principle plays out spiritually, too. In the busyness of our days, it's always easier to feed on sources of cheap nourishment like social media, news, TV shows, movies, and even superficial relationships, rather than Scripture. While it might be okay to engage in these things once in a while, we cannot expect to receive nourishment from them. They won't satisfy our spirit or strengthen our soul like God's Word does! Feeding on Scripture constantly keeps us healthy and growing into the mature believers God has called us to be.

GOD'S WORD IS FUEL FOR OUR SPIRIT AND NOURISHMENT FOR OUR SOULS!

I'm reminded of this truth when feeding my one-year-old daughter, Emma. She's in the teething stage right now, so chewing is her biggest hobby! One of her favorite teething toys is shaped like a cute avocado. When she's in pain, it provides temporary relief, but if she's hungry, it just becomes a distraction. She wants the *real* thing!

In life, we'll all experience pain and trauma that will try to persuade us toward temporary relief, but none of these things will compare to the lasting nourishment we receive and the continual growth we experience from feeding on God's Word. And like a baby, the more we mature, the more we need to sustain ourselves. That's why 1 Peter 2:2-3 says, "Like newborn babies, crave pure spiritual milk, so that by it you may grow up in your salvation, now that you have tasted that the Lord is good."

Although Scripture is crystal clear about the crucial nature of God's Word, there are still some who don't think studying it on their own is necessary. I have spoken with people of all ages and stages of their faith journey who feel this way. Usually, they take one of three stances.

The first is, *I've been reading the Word for years. Why should I keep reading it if I already know it so well?* Well, first, we don't stop eating when we become an adult, do we? No! We continue to eat so that our bodies can remain strong and healthy. Second, no matter how much Scripture we have read, God promises to reveal new things to us continually. Every time we read, we can expect fresh revelation, strengthened faith, and fuel added to the fire of God in our lives.

Another argument is, *Isn't that the pastor's job? I learn much better when someone teaches the Word to me.* Friend, this is not enough! Just like you can't simply eat once a week and stay alive, one Sunday sermon per week cannot carry us through the other six days. We must spend our *own* time in God's Word daily, and we must meditate on it throughout our day. If you're worried about the amount of time reading God's Word takes, start with fifteen minutes per day. You can even use the YouVersion Bible app to download reading plans, and you can turn on the audio feature to listen to Scripture while you drive, work out, or do chores around the house. There is no excuse for *not* spending time in The Word!

The third argument I hear is *It's just too hard to understand Scripture! I feel like I am wasting my time.* If this is how you feel, please know that I understand how overwhelming it can seem, especially when you're just starting. But know this, too: you live in an incredible time in history, with so much knowledge at your fingertips. So, make the most of it! Invest in a study Bible, concordance, and commentary, or simply download these apps for your smartphone.

One thing I love most about the invaluable nature of God's Word is that when we read it, it reads us, too. Hebrews 4:12 says:

> *For the word of God is alive and active. Sharper than any double-edged sword, it penetrates even to dividing soul and spirit, joints and marrow; it judges the thoughts and attitudes of the heart.*

God's Word is operative, powerful, and energizing. It corrects us, directs us, and empowers us. Studying it and meditating on it has completely changed my life for the best. It has helped me to stay fresh and flourishing in every season, and I know it will do the same for you.

WHEN WE READ GOD'S WORD, IT READS US, TOO.

Say it Out Loud

Fourteen years ago, after my dad passed away, I began experiencing strange health problems. One day, while traveling, I had what I thought was a heart attack. I went straight to the hospital, only to find that it *wasn't* a heart attack. It was a stress attack.

For the next month, I continued to experience these moments of anxiety. My doctor recommended finding natural ways to de-stress.

One day, I desperately asked God for wisdom to get to the root of the issue. He gently impressed on my heart something I didn't see coming. God showed me that when I lost my dad, I began doubting His goodness. I questioned whether He would take care of me and be good to me. Instead of operating from a spirit of faith, I was operating from a spirit of fear. *This* was causing the anxiety.

As I prayed these realities through, God dealt with me about two things. First, He showed me I was basing my faith on the experience of losing my dad, not on the authority of His Word. God's Word *alone* has the final say! Jesus is a healer, and He is the same yesterday, today, and forever. We can put our faith in His promises to heal, save, and deliver, no matter the circumstance! The second thing He dealt with me about was renewing my mind. He reminded me of the truth in Romans 10:17 (NKJV) that says, ". . . So then faith comes by hearing, and hearing by the word of God."

In response to my conversation with God that day, I wrote out scriptures dealing with anxiety. I meditated on these verses daily, reminding myself of His purpose, plan, goodness, and love for me. I fed on His faithfulness with passages like Philippians 4:6-8 which says:

> *Do not be anxious about anything, but in every situation, by prayer and petition, with thanksgiving, present your requests to God. And the peace of God, which transcends all under-standing, will guard your hearts and your minds in Christ Jesus. Finally, brothers and sisters, whatever is true, whatever is noble, whatever is right, whatever is pure, whatever is lovely, whatever*

*is admirable—if anything is excellent or praiseworthy—think
about such things.*

One of my go-to verses was Isaiah 26:3-4, which says, "You will keep
in perfect peace those whose minds are steadfast, because they
trust in you. Trust in the Lord forever, for the Lord, the Lord himself,
is the Rock eternal." Another was 2 Timothy 1:7 which says, "For the
Spirit God gave us does not make us timid, but gives us power, love
and self-discipline."

GOD'S WORD IS OPERATIVE, POWERFUL, AND ENERGIZING. IT CORRECTS US, DIRECTS US, AND EMPOWERS US.

I didn't just read these passages, though. I spoke them, too. This
made all the difference! 2 Corinthians 4:13 says, "It is written: 'I
believed; therefore I have spoken.' Since we have that same spirit
of faith, we also believe and therefore speak . . . " When we not
only meditate on God's promises by reading but also by speaking
them out loud, God's words come alive in our hearts.

The more I spoke these passages, the more faith rose in my spirit,
and the more my perspective transformed. As I planted the seed of
God's Word in my heart by speaking it out loud, and took authority

over the lies of the enemy, the anxiety dissipated. I grew stronger in my belief that God loves me, is for me, and has great plans for my life—plans for me to flourish in *every* season, no matter what that season looks like. Thank God, this all happened over thirteen years ago now, and I've not had a stress attack since! As 1 John 4:18 says, "God's perfect love drives out fear!"

GOD'S WORD ALONE HAS THE FINAL SAY!

Another beautiful example of the importance of speaking God's Word is one of a mom—Caroline—who desperately needed a miracle for her son, Jonathan.

Jonathan was an athletic 16-year-old track star with a scholarship to run in college. It surprised him and his whole family when their doctor found cancer in one of his knees. It shocked them even more when he was told his leg needed to be amputated. Thankfully, Caroline, Jonathan, and their whole family were deeply rooted in the Word, so they held on to God's promises, praying, seeking agreement with other believers, and speaking the Word over the situation. Jonathan's family even started calling him "Jonathan new knees" as a faith declaration that God was going to heal him.

I was a youth pastor at our church during this time, so Caroline asked me to visit their home to pray for Jonathan. When I did, I saw Scripture passages all over the house. There were healing songs playing. This family was believing for a miracle, and they wouldn't allow anyone to speak against it! Hour after hour, day after day, they planted seeds of God's Word, faith, encouragement, and prayer.

Those seeds sprouted, and two weeks later, the family received their harvest. Jonathan returned for a checkup, and the doctor confirmed what they believed: he was healed! The cancer was gone! Today, Jonathan continues to serve God and fulfill His purpose with no sickness.

You may or may not be in need of physical healing today, but we all have areas in our lives in which we need some type of healing, direction, or changed perspective. We all have areas in which we aren't flourishing. What are yours? I encourage you to search the Word for God's promises in that area. Then, write them out and speak them *out loud* every day. Meditate on them as food for your spirit and don't settle for the counterfeit! (Turn to Appendix C for some ideas!) My life is proof that if you'll feed your faith and starve your fears, you *will* see a radical transformation. The seed of God's Word will sprout, producing the most beautiful, flourishing fruit of God's Spirit.

From the Inside Out

When comparing what we plant in our hearts to seeds, it's important to notice how a seed grows. It doesn't grow from the bottom to the top; it grows from the inside out. One of my favorite stories that proves this comes from a friend in my home church. You'll read a more detailed account of her story at the end of this chapter.

Years ago, Tara hit rock bottom. She had been thrown in jail for selling illegal drugs. She felt hopeless knowing she was so far off track but thank God He knows no distance! He always meets us right where we are. One night, while sitting in her cell, Jesus physically appeared to her. Overcome with the emotion of having the Savior in her presence, she fell to her knees, repented, and surrendered her life to Him.

But she didn't stop there. From that day on, she planted seeds of God's Word in her heart. Someone gave her a Bible, and she threw herself into reading it like a hungry baby desperately feeding on milk. She devoured all the truth she could from Scripture, planting the promises of God deep in the surrendered soil of her heart. One night in particular, she remembers praying, "God, I want to do what *you* want me to do. I want to go where *you* want me to go. Take control of my life."

As she continued to plant and nurture these seeds of God's Word, they sprouted in the most incredible of ways. She was released from jail earlier than expected. When she got out, she attended Bible school and became majorly involved in church. God brought her an amazing husband, and now they have a beautiful family. They're in ministry today, daily bringing hope and healing to others.

What a transformation! But notice—this incredible change didn't start on the outside. It started on the inside. My friend consistently planted seeds of God's Word deep in her heart, and eventually, they took root and sprouted. She spoke God's promises over her life, and they became a reality. She *flourished*.

Friends, God's Word works. No matter where you've been or what you've done, I urge you to treasure the power of the seed of God's Word. Prioritize it, protect it, and nurture it. When you do, God's goodness and faithfulness *will* follow in abundance!

Questions for Reflection:

1) What are some of the ways Scripture describes God's Word? Write them out with the reference next to them. (Ex. Active— Hebrews 4:12)

_____

_____

_____

_____

_____

_____

_____

_____

2) Is studying the Bible a habit for you? If not, do you relate to any of the excuses presented in this chapter? Which one(s)?

_____

_____

_____

_____

_____

_____

_____

_____

3) Where is the first place you turn when you're in need of comfort or advice? If it's not the Bible, how can you remind yourself to turn to Scripture before anything else?

_____

_____

_____

_____

_____

_____

_____

_____

_____

_____

_____

_____

_____

_____

_____

_____

Passage for Further Study:

Isaiah 55:10-11

Call to Action:

Write your plan for studying God's Word. Make it one you'll stick to! If you're just beginning, start with ten to fifteen minutes in the morning or before you go to bed. Then, increase your time as it becomes a habit. Also, include what resources you'll need—a study Bible, apps, concordances—whatever will help you gain the most from your time. Finally, show up. Engage in the daily practice of Bible study until it becomes a habit. You'll be so glad you did!

_____

_____

_____

_____

_____

_____

_____

_____

_____

_____

_____

_____

_____

_____

_____

_____

Prayer for Today:

Lord,

Thank you for the gift of your Word and for the freedom to study it. Help me to steward my time so that I prioritize seeking the wisdom, guidance, and strength presented in its pages. Help me make studying and speaking your Word a habit. Then, give me the grace to allow it to work in my life, changing me from the inside out.

In Jesus' name,

Amen

Story of Flourishing:

I grew up knowing that everyone around my mother wanted her to have an abortion—her parents, the father, and the doctor. Thankfully, my mother refused. She went to live in another town, with a family she didn't know, so that she could join a Christian organization helping with unplanned pregnancies. Praise God for His hand and protection in my life from the beginning!

Still, I wasn't raised in a Christian home. This, on top of not having a father present, led me to victimize myself, turning to drugs and alcohol to numb my pain. By 15, I was living on the streets, and by 17, I was manufacturing meth and other drugs. I was in and out of juvenile detention and jail over thirty-two times. I was certified as an adult at 17, then kicked out of multiple programs.

This estranged me from my mother for nine years. During this time, she gave herself fully to the Lord. She tried to encourage me to do the same, but I resisted. Finally, one day, my mother had enough. She gave up trying to change me in her own efforts and, in prayer, released me to the Lord. Days later, on September 6th, 2005, I was incarcerated for the last time. The FBI ran in on me after watching me for two years. I faced 25 years in prison, but God!

A couple of weeks later—on September 22nd—Jesus Christ appeared to me in my jail cell. I gave my life to Him that day, and He began unfolding the plan He had for me. I started making changes right away, planting seeds of God's Word and His dreams for me deep in my heart. Shortly after this, I was released from jail. I kept living for Jesus, and within a year, I began returning to that same jail to minister. Today, my husband and I both run with the fire that fell in my cell that day. We live to set the captives free and preach the gospel to all.

—Tara

Chapter Four

TEND THE SOIL

Keep your heart with all vigilance, for from it flow
the springs of life. —Proverbs 4:23 (ESV)

J ust as there are many types of seed a farmer can plant, there are also many types of soil he can plant in. No matter how much potential a seed has, unless it's planted in *good* soil, that potential becomes irrelevant.

It's the same in our walks of faith. There are many types of seed we can plant, but the most important will always be the seed of God's Word. No matter how much potential it has to produce beauty in our lives, though, that potential becomes irrelevant if our heart-soil is not good. Jesus makes this clear in the Parable of the Sower in Matthew 13:3-9 and 18-23 (NLT). The passage reads:

> . . . A farmer went out to plant some seeds. As he scattered them across his field, some seeds fell on a footpath, and the birds came and ate them. Other seeds fell on shallow soil with underlying rock. The seeds sprouted quickly because the soil was shallow. But the plants soon wilted under the hot sun,

and since they didn't have deep roots, they died. Other seeds fell among thorns that grew up and choked out the tender plants. Still other seeds fell on fertile soil, and they produced a crop that was thirty, sixty, and even a hundred times as much as had been planted! Anyone with ears to hear should listen and understand.

The passage continues:

Now, listen to the explanation of the parable about the farmer planting seeds: The seed that fell on the footpath represents those who hear the message about the Kingdom and don't understand it. Then the evil one comes and snatches away the seed that was planted in their hearts. The seed on the rocky soil represents those who hear the message and immediately receive it with joy. But since they don't have deep roots, they don't last long. They fall away as soon as they have problems or are persecuted for believing God's word. The seed that fell among the thorns represents those who hear God's word, but all too quickly the message is crowded out by the worries of this life and the lure of wealth, so no fruit is produced. The seed that fell on good soil represents those who truly hear and understand God's word and produce a harvest of thirty, sixty, or even a hundred times as much as had been planted!

Planting God's Word in healthy, receptive heart-soil will set our lives up to flourish. It will produce sweet, bountiful fruit, such as peace, joy, purpose, and confidence in our identity. This is why James 1:21

(NLT) tells us to "humbly accept the word God has planted in your hearts, for it has the power to save your souls."

Tending our heart-soil is vital to flourishing, but just like a farmer in his field, it's work. In the Parable of the Sower, Jesus highlights this, teaching us about three kinds of heart-soil that threaten to steal our harvest.

Same Seed, Different Soil

The first type He mentions is pathway soil. Here, the sower plants seed with gladness, but later, birds steal it because it has not gone deep enough. This type of soil represents a heart who receives God's Word with joy. But when the enemy comes to snatch that Word—those promises—from their heart, he succeeds because this person did not pursue understanding. He did not tend his heart-soil so that the seed could go deep.

The second type of soil is shallow, rocky soil. The seeds in this soil sprouted, but the plants wilted under the sun's heat. Why? Because the soil never gave space for the seed to develop roots. This type of soil represents a heart that hears the Word and receives it but doesn't fully believe it. When trouble comes, the plant that had flourished ceases because it did not take root.

The third type of soil is thorny soil. In this soil, thorns grew alongside the plants and choked them out. The thorny soil represents those who hear the Word and receive it. However, they later allow distractions like worry and lust to destroy the blessing God was trying to grow. All three soils destroy the potential of the seed.

The last type of heart soil Jesus mentions is the good soil. This type of soil is fertile, producing a bountiful harvest. The good soil represents those who hear and receive God's Word, seek to understand it, believe it, and avoid the distractions that keep their harvest from flourishing. We want *this* to be our heart-soil.

THE WORD HAS INCREDIBLE POWER, BUT THE FRUIT WE BEAR DEPENDS ON THE RECEPTIVITY OF OUR HEARTS.

One of my favorite parts of the Parable of the Sower is the fact that each soil received the *same* seed. One seed had no more potential than another. So, success depended on more than just the seed that was received. It also depended on the tending of the soil. In the same way, the Word has incredible power, but the fruit we bear still depends on the receptivity of our hearts.

I love this because on our faith journey, it puts the ball in our court, so to speak. *We* get to choose how much we flourish by how well we tend our heart-soil. Proverbs 4:23 says, "Above all else, guard your heart, for everything you do flows from it." So how do we get—and keep—our heart soil healthy? We receive the Word with gladness, seek to understand it, believe it, and keep up with the weeds.

Keep Up With the Weeds

Just like a farmer has to constantly pull weeds that threaten his crop, we have to regularly pull weeds from the soil of our hearts. We must pull weeds of doubt, worry, resentment, lust, comparison, judgment, and greed—just to name a few! We do this so that God's Word can have the freedom to grow and produce abundant fruit in our lives.

FORGIVENESS HELPS YOU FLOURISH.

One weed that will constantly try to grow in the soil of every believer's heart is the weed of offense. Life in our fallen world offers daily opportunities for this. We can either choose to forgive, pulling that weed of offense from our heart-soil, or we can choose to hold on to that offense, allowing it to form a root of bitterness and eventually choke out our harvest.

Friend, *forgiveness* will always be a major key to *flourishing*. I know this because I have experienced it. People close to me have betrayed me, and it hurt deeply because I loved them and trusted them. I know that to keep moving forward with God, I *must* forgive those who hurt me, even if they never apologize. Then, I must go a step further, blessing them, too.

Usually, I bless them by speaking good things over their lives, but a few times, God has impressed on me to go a step further and send a gift to them. I did not always want to do that, but I knew God wanted me to for my own good. So, I did. In the months that followed, I reaped such incredible fruit in my life! I know it was because of His graciousness in leading me and my obedience in tending my heart's soil.

Luke 6:27-28 (NKJV) says, " . . . Love your enemies, do good to those who hate you, bless those who curse you, and pray for those who spitefully use you." When we trust God in forgiving offenses, He fights for us, pursuing our vindication, while our seed continues to flourish.

Now, I'll be honest with you: this sounds great, but it's not easy. It's not easy to pull thoughts of disappointment from your mind every time you recall a hurtful situation. It's not easy to pull weeds of offense from your heart every time you see the person who has hurt you. But when you commit to tending your soil through forgiveness and graciousness, you create *good* soil in which a beautiful life can flourish.

Weeds have a way of hiding, though. That's because the enemy doesn't want you to walk in freedom, joy, and purpose, so he will do everything possible to keep you from seeing the weeds or rationalizing their existence. In order to stay flourishing, we must regularly ask God to point the weeds out to us. We should ask daily, "Is there anything I need to pull from my soil today? What needs to be removed so that your Word can produce good fruit?"

Sometimes the weeds of offense He points out will be ones we thought we already got rid of. That's because forgiveness isn't always a one-time thing. Often, when memories resurface, the hurt does, too. We must continue to pull those weeds and trust in God to defend us.

Now listen, I realize you may have endured horrific things in your life that no one should ever have to endure. If so, please know I am *not* minimizing what you've gone through. I am only seeking to encourage you to let go of offense for the sake of your *own* harvest. For *your* future, give up bitterness. It's simply not worth it, because it will choke out the good things God wants to grow in your life. *Forgiveness* helps you *flourish*.

As English poet William Wordsworth said, "Your mind is a garden. Your thoughts are the seeds. You can grow flowers, or you can grow weeds."[4] What will you allow to grow in your garden? Fear or faith? Bitterness or forgiveness? Greed or generosity? Jealousy or contentment? God is good and faithful to redeem *every* hurtful, terrible thing that has happened to you. He longs to be good to you! Will you trust Him to help you tend your heart-soil?

---

4 Sharon Packer, MD, "Weeds, Wildflowers, and Wordsworth," Psychiatric Times, February 4, 2022, https://www.psychiatrictimes.com/view/weeds-wildflowers-and-wordsworth.

Questions for Reflection:

1) Which of the four types of heart-soil do you think you currently have? Why?

_____

_____

_____

_____

_____

_____

_____

_____

_____

2) Are there weeds that need to be pulled from the soil of your heart? If so, what are they?

_____

_____

_____

_____

_____

_____

_____

_____

3) Why is the Bible clear that guarding our hearts is a personal responsibility?

_____

_____

_____

_____

_____

_____

_____

_____

_____

_____

_____

_____

_____

_____

_____

_____

Passage for Further Study:
Ephesians 4:31-32

Call to Action:

Take a moment to think about whether you are harboring unfor-giveness toward anyone in your past or present. If you are unsure, ask the Holy Spirit to bring them to mind. Then, release them to God. Forgive them and commit to continually doing so. If you need help identifying other types of weeds keeping you stuck, check out my book *Advance: Living Unstuck and Moving Forward in Faith*. It will help you identify and remove what's holding you back so that you can flourish in all God has for you.

_____

_____

_____

_____

_____

_____

_____

_____

_____

_____

_____

_____

_____

_____

_____

Prayer for Today:

Father,

Thank you for your promise of flourishing in every area and in every season of life. Please help me discover what in my heart-soil might be keeping me from walking into the future you have for me. When you show me, help me to uproot it with confidence and strength, never turning back to what held me down. I surrender all that I am to you, inviting your Holy Spirit to have His way in my life.

In Jesus' name,

Amen

Story of Flourishing:

When I was approaching my sophomore year of high school, the love of Jesus and the power of His Holy Spirit radically changed my life. I grew up without a father, which meant not having the affirmation, love, provision, and security a girl needs to thrive. I struggled with depression, loss of self-worth, and a lack of identity, which led to contemplating suicide several times. It seemed I searched for the love I was missing in relationships that would instead lead to more heartbreak.

It wasn't until I heard the message of Jesus that my life found meaning. I was told that God loved me and had a plan for me. I believed what He said, and I surrendered my life to Him. He started bringing people into my life to help me learn how to follow Jesus.

When I rid my heart of things that didn't line up with His Word, my life began to flourish. Depression, anger, and heaviness melted away as I allowed the Father to change me from the inside out. He helped me to forgive those who hurt and abandoned me. As I did, His healing flooded my life, and with it, His freedom and peace. I know that He will do the same for anyone who surrenders their hurt to Him.

—Star

Chapter Five
SOW THE SEED

Remember this: Whoever sows sparingly will also
reap sparingly, and whoever sows generously will
also reap generously. —2 Corinthians 9:6

W e've talked about the most important seed we can plant—
God's Word. But there are other seeds we can plant, too.
Three types God calls us to sow regularly are seeds of time, talent,
and treasure.

Time

In some circumstances, God will lead us to sow seeds of time. He
will ask us to give of our schedule to plant seeds of blessing into our
futures and into the futures of those around us.

I remember when He asked this of one of my friends. She and her
husband had recently become parents and were believing for friend-
ship with like-minded believers in a similar season. This friend often
struggled with bouts of loneliness while she waited for God to bring

her these relationships. Then, one day, God said to her, "Stop waiting for people to invite you. *You* invite them!" So she did.

My friend and her husband started a small group for couples in their home. They invested time in communicating with this group, preparing food for them, and hosting them. Again, it didn't happen right away, but as my friend and her husband sowed these seeds of time, they reaped a beautiful harvest of joy and purpose-filled relationships they still treasure to this day.

God has asked the same of me throughout various seasons. I'll never forget one time in particular. I was a freshman in college when I shared with my dad that I felt called to a life working in ministry. His response was, "That's great, Sarah. If that's where you know your life is headed, then start here, and start now." He then asked me to fill a position that had just opened within our home church—the role of a weekend children's pastor for a new service.

My first thought was, *There's no way. I'm a college student taking a full course load. I have two part-time campus jobs. I have so many other things to keep up with. I don't think I have the time!* Those were my *thoughts*, but the *words* I spoke back to my dad that day were, "Okay, Dad. Just let me pray about it."

Over the next few days, I sought God about whether this was the right thing for me, and I felt strongly that it was. So, I accepted the position. Every week, I sowed seeds of time into those children. It wasn't always easy, but it proved worth it, not just for the kids, but for me, too. God built things in me during that season that have continually helped me walk out His purposes for my life. Because of that step of obedience, God opened up other doors of ministry that prepared me for what I am doing now. As it always does when we obey God, the harvest proved well worth that season of sowing.

Another example of sowing seeds of time is when I was in the thick of serving as a youth pastor, teaching and training young people to know, love, and serve God. To be honest, many days, it felt like I was wasting my time. Most of the teens didn't seem interested, and they certainly did not seem grateful.

One day, I was feeling especially discouraged and decided I wanted to quit. So I went to God in prayer. As much as I wanted Him to give me the green light to change seasons, He didn't. Instead, He responded, "Sarah, you're in a season of sowing seeds. You are where you're supposed to be. You will not see the harvest right away, but I promise: it *is* coming. It just takes time."

I'm so grateful for God's leadership in my life. After my conversation with Him that day, I committed to sticking with pastoring that youth group for the five years I was asked to lead it. Though I certainly still had times I *wanted* to quit, I didn't, and I'm glad I didn't. Later, an opportunity opened for me to lead the church's missions department and young adults ministry, and I knew it was the right time to transition.

It's been 20 years since then, and I *still* receive direct messages and emails from people who were in that youth group. They always express their gratitude, explaining how things I said, lessons they learned, and experiences they had during that time have helped to shape their life. Today, kids from this youth group fill many of the key pastoral roles of our church. It is a joy to watch them pursue God with such passion and live out their purpose daily. Those seeds of time truly sprouted an incredible harvest!

Talent

Another type of seed God will often ask us to sow are seeds of talent. He has given us all various gifts, but they were not given to us only for our own enjoyment. They were also given to serve others and to build God's Kingdom! His heart is that we use what He has blessed us with to bless others. We were not saved *by* good works; instead, Ephesians 2:10 says we were created *for* good works! We were created to plant seeds of talent that bring a harvest of glory to God.

You might think, *But Sarah, I don't have any major talents or spiritual gifts. I can't sing or play an instrument, and I am way too scared to talk in front of people.* Please don't think God can only use talents displayed onstage or on screen. That could not be further from the truth! Throughout Scripture, we see He uses both talents and spiritual gifts of all kinds.

While we may be more familiar with our talents, we should not ignore our spiritual gifts. Romans 12:6-8 encourages us about them when it says:

We have different gifts, according to the grace given to each of us. If your gift is prophesying, then prophesy in accordance with your faith; if it is serving, then serve; if it is teaching, then teach; if it is to encourage, then give encouragement; if it is giving, then give generously; if it is to lead, do it diligently; if it is to show mercy, do it cheerfully.

1 Corinthians 12:7-10 gives more examples. It mentions the spiritual gifts of wisdom, faith, healing, discernment, tongues, and more. Verse eleven ends the passage by saying, "All these are the work of one and the same Spirit, and he distributes them to each one, just as he determines." So, God uses all kinds of spiritual gifts. And the best part? He doesn't just pick the people we consider to have the strongest gifts. We *all* have a vital part to play in planting seeds of our gifts and talents for a Kingdom-harvest.

This reminds me of my grandmother, who has the gift of encouragement. She really struggled when my grandfather passed away, so one day, my dad encouraged her to use her gift of encouragement to sow seeds of hope and healing for others. The next week, she began visiting people in nursing homes, praying over them, and encouraging them in their season. To this day, she'll say she reaped a harvest of joy when she sowed seeds of encouragement in others.

What gifts and talents has God given you? Like my grandmother, do you love encouraging others? Are you organized? Do you love caring for children? Whatever your gifts and talents are, I encourage you, like my dad encouraged my grandmother—get out there and use them! As you do, you will undoubtedly reap a great harvest.

If you are struggling to find your talents, I urge you to spend time praying about it. After all, God is your Creator! He knows exactly what He put in you, and He promises to speak to you when you seek Him. You can also ask a friend or a mentor—someone who knows you well and in whom you can trust. Personality tests and spiritual gifts tests are also a helpful tool in discerning the gifts and talents God has given you. You can take a free one online at www.biblesprout.com/articles/god/holy-spirit/spiritual-gifts-test/. Don't allow the enemy to convince you that you don't have anything significant to plant in this area. *Your* gifts and talents matter!

Treasure

The third type of seed God will often ask us to sow are seeds of treasure. I have experienced this urging in my life many times. When I submitted to it, sowing what I had, God brought an abundant harvest at the most perfect times.

When our oldest two children were toddlers, Caleb and I moved our family to Hong Kong to establish mission work there. God had given us a dream of reaching people, helping orphans, and building water wells. This was a *huge* step of faith for us. The plans all felt so big—too big, most days. It was a constant choice to walk by faith.

One of the areas it was easiest to grow discouraged in was our finances. Although we started saving money the day God spoke to us and had believed for His provision for months, we still only saved enough money to get by for a couple of months in Hong Kong. We desperately needed God's provision!

WHEN IN NEED, PLANT A SEED!

Right before we left, He spoke to us, but His instruction was not what we expected! God asked us to sow a significant financial seed into five ministries who were doing the very things we were believing for Him to do through us. It made no sense in the natural. We needed that money! Thankfully, though, we understood the principle of sowing and reaping. So, we sowed the seed, giving all that we had saved.

Sure enough, that planting set the harvest in motion. God answered our prayers. He spoke to people we hardly knew to give money toward our outreaches. Once we moved to Hong Kong, He provided us with jobs at our home church there. He also provided for us to complete the outreaches He had put on our hearts. Today, we have built thirty-one children's homes, five schools, and one hundred seventy-five water wells throughout Southeast Asia, and the list keeps growing. It's miraculous what God has done!

Since then, when I find a part of my life lacking, I remind myself of the miracles God performed for us throughout that season. In fact, now, I often teach others that, "When in need, plant a seed!"

Why? Because it's often when you feel you don't have enough to give, that you need to plant your seed the most. My life is proof that if you obey, you'll stand in awe of the supernatural harvest God brings, even in the most dire circumstances.

My life doesn't just prove this truth, though. Scripture does, too. Genesis 26:1, 12-33 tells us that Isaac sowed seed during a severe famine, and in that same year, he reaped a hundredfold! God blessed him tremendously when things looked terrible. In fact, Scripture says that he was so blessed that people began growing jealous of him! In verse twenty-two, we find that Isaac named the land of his fruitfulness "Rehoboth" which means "room."[5] He gratefully declared, ". . . Now the LORD has given us room and we will flourish in the land."

YOUR JOB IS TO PLANT AND WAIT IN FAITH. GOD'S JOB IS TO BRING THE HARVEST.

Friends, where do you need room to flourish? I firmly believe that it's your time. As Ephesians 3:20 says, God is "able to do immeasurably more than all we ask or imagine," but we must trust Him to the point of action.

5 "What Does Genesis 26:22 Mean?," BibleRef.com, accessed January 23, 2023, https://www.bibleref.com/Genesis/26/Genesis-26-22.html#:~:text=He%20names%20this%20well%\20Rehoboth,of%20all%20of%20his%20possessions.

The truth is that what you have will never be enough to bring God's dream for your life to pass. The good news is that it doesn't have to be. *Your* job is to plant and wait in faith. *God's* job is to bring the harvest, and He *always* comes through.

Seedtime and Harvest

The sowing and reaping process has three stages: planting the seed, waiting for the harvest, and reaping the harvest. It has always been this way, and it always will be. Genesis 8:22 talks about two of these when it says, "As long as the earth endures, seedtime and harvest, cold and heat, summer and winter, day and night will never cease."

So, the *seed* is where it all begins. After we plant it in faith, then comes the second part in the process: *time*. We must wait patiently, remaining confident that the harvest is on its way. In my life, the second part has always been the hardest. That's because we can't hurry this process along. It simply takes time.

The interesting thing about this phase is that every person's journey is different. A waiting season for one person could be five weeks, and for another person, it could be five years. However long the waiting season for our harvest is, we must trust that God knows how long we need to grow a bountiful harvest we will reap at the perfect time for us.

This waiting season is *NOT* one of inaction, though. Throughout it, we need to fertilize the seed, care for it, and remain vigilant against weeds and other threats to our harvest. Practically, this looks like spending time in God's Word daily, praying for God to lead us, and obeying when He does. It looks like joining a local church, connecting with like-minded believers, and serving in God's House.

SEEDS PLANTED AND NURTURED IN FAITH ALWAYS PRODUCE AN ABUNDANT HARVEST.

It also looks like aligning our words and actions with God's Word. When we get discouraged by the lack of growth we see with our natural eyes, we've got to look at our fields with supernatural eyes. Then, we've got to speak what we supernaturally see. It may take time, but seeds planted and nurtured in faith *always* produce an abundant harvest.

In Isaiah 55:10-11, God promises us:

> *As the rain and the snow come down from heaven, and do not return to it without watering the earth and making it bud and flourish, so that it yields seed for the sower and bread for the eater, so is my word that goes out from my mouth: It will not return to me empty, but will accomplish what I desire and achieve the purpose for which I sent it.*

What area in your life are you believing to flourish? I encourage you to spend time today thinking about what seeds you can plant, even when you feel you have nothing to give. Then trust that your seed *today* will bring a harvest *tomorrow!*

Questions for Reflection:

1) How has God asked you to sow seeds of time in the past? What about talent? Treasure?

_____

_____

_____

_____

_____

_____

_____

2) Return to chapter two, question one. Regarding the dreams you wrote down, how might you plant seeds of time, talent, and treasure toward your harvest? If you haven't taken a strengths test or spiritual gifts test, those are great ideas to help you discover your gifts and talents. There are a lot of free assessments online you can access and one spiritual gifts test that is free that is mentioned in the chapter is: (www.biblesprout.com/articles/god/holy-spirit/spiritual-gifts-test/) Another idea could be to check out a book on the topic. Some of my favorites are *Discovering and Activating my Spiritual Gifts* by Havilah Cunnington and *The Gifts and Ministries of the Holy Spirit* by Dr. Lester Sumrall.

_____

_____

_____

_____

_____

_____

_____

_____

_____

_____

_____

3) What part of the sowing and reaping process do you feel you are in right now? Planting time, waiting time, or harvest time? How can you remain faithful in that season?

_____

_____

_____

_____

_____

_____

_____

_____

_____

_____

_____

Passage for Further Study:

Galatians 6:7-9

Call to Action:

Take the ideas from your answer in question two and write out a plan to implement them. Remember—even small seeds of time, talent, and treasure planted in faith will reap a great harvest. Now, sow in faith, believing that every seed you sow will bring a harvest!

_____

_____

_____

_____

_____

_____

_____

_____

_____

_____

_____

_____

_____

_____

_____

_____

Prayer for Today:

Lord,

I thank you that your Word never returns void. Thank you that you always bring a harvest from the seeds we plant. Father, I ask that you open my eyes and heart to know where, what, when, and how you would have me plant my seeds. Then, I ask you to give me the wisdom to follow through, and the grace to wait confidently for my harvest.

In Jesus' name,

Amen

Story of Flourishing:

Many young ministers expect their dreams to be fulfilled quickly upon discovering their calling to full-time ministry. These unrealistic expectations can create major roadblocks along our journey. I was one of these young people! On December 5, 1994, I came to the States from the former communist country of Bulgaria. At nineteen years old, I came with only two suitcases, one hundred dollars in my pocket, and one hundred words of English in my vocabulary.

I was both scared and excited to begin my studies at a Bible college in Tulsa, Oklahoma. My goal was to become a preacher and establish a nonprofit to help underprivileged children in Bulgaria. I had convinced myself that by twenty-one years old, I needed to change the world, so I had no time to waste! No one could have prepared me for the journey ahead.

It's been twenty-eight years since those early beginnings, and although I may not have changed the entire world, I have helped brighten the worlds of those the Lord has brought into my life. I started supporting one orphan in Bulgaria with one dollar per month in 1995. It was the only seed I could afford to plant toward the dream God had given me. Still, although it was minimal, I believed the seed would sprout a harvest. And it did!

Over the years, the fruit of that seed has continually flourished. Today, our organization ministers to thousands of boys and girls each month through its many programs. I know if I had not planted those small seeds, I wouldn't have reaped the fruit I have now. In the waiting, I learned how to receive God's miracles, trust in His plan, and believe in His character.

—Ceitci

Chapter Six

MAKE ROOM FOR PRUNING

*I am the true vine, and my Father is the Gardner. He
cuts off every branch in me that bears no fruit, while
every branch that does bear fruit he prunes so that it
will be even more fruitful. —John 15:1-2 (GNT)*

I f you weren't before, you're now aware of the fact that a plant
goes through many processes on its way to flourishing. We've
talked about connecting, preparing, planting, and tending. These
will all get the harvest growing, but there's one process that is key
to its healthy growth for the long haul. It's the pruning process. I
know what you're probably thinking, *Pruning? Ugh! Let's skip to the
next chapter!*

Listen—I get it. Pruning doesn't sound fun. It sounds hard and
maybe even unnecessary. Though I won't say this process is enjoy-
able or easy, if you'll keep reading, I believe you'll be convinced of its
life-changing nature. I can say from experience that submitting to
God's pruning process is one of the best choices we can ever make.

It keeps life exciting and effective, helping us make progress and continually bear abundant fruit.

We mentioned John 15:1-8 in the first chapter. This passage proves how vital connecting to the source is, but it also shows the importance of pruning.

God will prune us whether we like it or not, so we might as well cooperate! Sometimes, we may feel like He's picking on us, but that's not His purpose in pruning at all. He simply knows our potential, and by His grace, is helping us get there. The encouraging fact is that despite how much fruit our lives are bearing today, we can always produce more. We've got to make a choice, though. We've got to choose to live surrendered to God, allowing Him to remove things that are holding us back from growth.

2 Corinthians 7:1 compares our surrender to another process—one of purifying precious metals. When a refiner wants to purify gold, he continually raises the heat to draw the dross (the scum) to the top. Then, he skims away that dross, bringing the gold to a higher level of purity. God does the same with us. 1 Peter 1:6-7 says:

> *In all this you greatly rejoice, though now for a little while you may have had to suffer grief in all kinds of trials. These have come so that the proven genuineness of your faith—of greater worth than gold, which perishes even though refined by fire—may result in praise, glory and honor when Jesus Christ is revealed.*

When we are walking through a tough time, we can trust that God is purifying us through it, preparing us for increase. Like a good metal refiner, He is removing things that are holding us back, so that we can be all He has called us to be.

GOD ONLY REMOVES TO MAKE ROOM FOR SOMETHING ELSE— SOMETHING BETTER FOR TODAY.

Some of the things He removes are sinful—like pride, jealousy, a wrong thought process, or a bad habit. Some things God removes aren't sinful at all. In fact, some things might have even been the right thing in one season; they're just wrong for the season we're walking into. If we keep them around, they'll hinder us from making progress. The writer of Hebrews calls this second type of hindrance "weights." Hebrews 12:1-2 (NLT) says:

> Therefore, since we are surrounded by such a huge crowd of witnesses to the life of faith, let us strip off every weight that slows us down, especially the sin that so easily trips us up. And let us run with endurance the race God has set before us. We do this by keeping our eyes on Jesus, the champion who initiates and perfects our faith. Because of the joy awaiting him, he endured the cross, disregarding its shame. Now he is seated in the place of honor beside God's throne.

To make progress in our lives, we must continually reassess what's in them, only allowing what will produce the *most* fruit to remain. In this part of the process, perspective makes all the difference. Instead of growing discouraged about what we're losing, we've got to look forward to what we'll gain. God is a loving Father, so we can trust He'll never take things away to hurt or frustrate us. He always does so to make room for something else—something better for *today*.

Make Space for the New

Every week, I purge my fridge and pantry. I take out what has expired or spoiled and replace it with fresh food for my family. I do the same thing with my kids' clothes. Every change-of-season, I declutter each of their closets, removing items that no longer fit them or their style, as well as items that were season-specific. Then, I fill their closet with new items—ones they like, ones that fit them well, and ones that are appropriate for the current season.

The picture of a closet clean-out helps us build a healthy perspective of the pruning process. When we take an honest look at our lives, we'll find some things that have to go. We may find garments of pride or fear, disappointment or anger. There might be pieces of past failures, present realities, or future worries threatening to choke our harvest. We may even discover once-great opportunities or once-appropriate activities are now just taking up space. In these moments, we must remember: we are not simply saying goodbye to things we may want to hold on to. We're making room for better things.

I can't stress enough the importance of seeking God throughout this process. Just like it's easy to see a nice piece in your closet and rationalize why you should keep it, it's easy to let good things stay in our lives and schedules just because they once served a meaningful purpose. These things may seem to fit, and it may even look like there's a spot on the shelf for them. But consider this—what better thing could you be saying no to, for fear of letting go?

God makes a strong point about pruning in Isaiah 43:18-19 (NKJV). He actually tells the Israelites to *forget* about the past! Through the prophet Isaiah, He said:

> *Do not remember the former things, nor consider the things of old. Behold, I will do a new thing, Now it shall spring forth; Shall you not know it? I will even make a road in the wilderness And rivers in the desert.*

Calling and Assignments

As you take time to declutter your life and schedule, there's another thing that's important to remember. While your purpose remains with you throughout your life, God will give you season-specific assignments. This is why it's so important to discern *your* unique purpose.

Discovering this purpose should not be stressful, as some make it out to be. As believers, we actually share much of the same purpose. We are called to love God first. Then we are called to love and serve our spouses, families, churches, and communities.

But God also gives us each unique callings, and our gifts match them. Maybe you love to teach people things, and you're good at it. Maybe you love to host events or organize or encourage. I urge you—as you seek God, ask Him to show you what gifts you have, and what purposes He has created you for. When you know your calling—what stays forever—you can more easily determine your current assignment.

I have experienced this truth in season after season. Though my calling to ministry has remained the same, my assignments in ministry have changed several times. I have served as a children's pastor, a youth pastor, a college pastor, and a missions director. My husband and I have helped plant churches, and I have even lived with my family as a missionary for a time. In each assignment, I knew I was to train someone else to do what I did because I likely wouldn't be in that role forever. My *calling* was the same, but my *assignments* changed.

Now, sometimes I wanted to switch assignments too soon. Like I mentioned in the previous chapter, when I was a youth pastor, there were times I wanted to give up. No matter how many times I prayed about it, though, God would never give me the green light to move on when I wanted to. Other times, I felt happy and fulfilled in my season. But just as my assignment began to flourish, God would say, "Okay, I have something new for you. Release that to someone else, and step into this." He would open a door, and I would know I needed to walk through it, as hard as it was to do so.

When we were newly married, Caleb and I began a college group at our church. Again, this season was one of consistent sowing. The college group took *years* to flourish. But finally, after five years of consistent sowing, it did. It seemed that overnight, it grew from a handful to hundreds. In that fifth year, we felt like we were finally bearing fruit. It was such a sweet season!

Even in our personal lives, everything seemed to be in a state of flourishing. We had a toddler and a baby on the way, and we had just bought a new house. We were so happy! But that fifth year, the Lord stirred in us that it was time to step out. In a worship service, I remember praying, "Lord, I feel I am doing all you've called me to do, but if there is anything else you'd like me to do, tell me. I am your girl." He then asked me the question, "Would you be willing to move to the mission field for the next season of your life?"

It didn't make a lot of sense in the natural because things seemed to be good on the outside. One day, in prayer, I asked God, *Why would you have us leave when things are going so well?* He responded, "If you don't step out in this new thing I'm calling you to, you'll grow stagnant in your faith, and you won't reach the people I am calling you to reach in the next season. Not only that, but you'll also hinder the work you started here."

That convicted me. I prayed, "Okay, God. I don't want to hinder anyone's growth—mine, the next leader's, or the peoples' that you've called me to. So, I submit to your process, but please tell my husband as well!" When I came home from that service, Caleb said he had noticed I was especially moved in worship that night.

He asked, "What did God tell you, Sarah?" At first, I didn't want to tell him, but after some convincing, I shared what I felt God had spoken to me.

My non-emotional husband began to cry. Then, he shared that God had spoken the same thing to him two weeks prior while he was in Asia coordinating an outreach. He knew we were called to go to that region for a season. It was not easy to let go of the familiar, but as we stepped out in faith, we flourished to an even greater degree than we had ever experienced before. God performed incredible miracles in and through our lives, and we saw multiplication from seeds we had planted years prior. Now, was pastoring a college ministry a *bad* thing? Absolutely not! It was *wonderful*, and it was our assignment for a season. However, when God brought something new, we had to make room for it.

THE KEY TO MAKING ROOM IS HEARING AND OBEYING THE VOICE OF GOD.

Friend, what do you need to lay aside to move forward into the new? Offense? Jealousy? Worry? Guilt? Or, are there weights you need to rid your life of? Are you filling your schedule with things that were once the right things, but aren't anymore? Be encouraged: we serve a BIG God—One for whom nothing is impossible. He wants to do more in your life, but you've got to make space for it!

The key to making room will always be hearing God and obeying what He says. So, take time to seek God. Ask Him what you need to lay aside so you can accept the new things He is bringing. Then, obey. Make room for the new. Though this cycle never ends as long as we're on earth, it does get easier with time, as we enjoy the result of flourishing in every season!

Questions for Reflection:

1) Think of a time God pruned something from your life. What was He making room for?

_____

_____

_____

_____

_____

_____

_____

_____

2) Ask God what you might need pruned from your life today. Take time to listen and write the answers.

_____

_____

_____

_____

_____

_____

_____

_____

3) Now, ask Him what He wants to add to your life in place of what He has removed. Write this answer in the journal space provided, next to the answers from question two.

_____

_____

_____

_____

_____

_____

_____

_____

_____

_____

_____

_____

_____

_____

_____

_____

_____

Passage for Further Study:
Hebrews 12:6-11 (MSG)

Call to Action:

Set regular time in your schedule to seek God about what in your life might need to be removed and replaced. If you need help discerning what the Lord is saying, grab my devotional and online study, *How to Hear God's Voice*. I believe it will help you in discerning the voice of God and in walking out the purpose He has for your life!

_____

_____

_____

_____

_____

_____

_____

_____

_____

_____

_____

_____

_____

_____

_____

_____

_____

_____

_____

Prayer for Today:

Lord,

Thank you for your promise to do exceedingly and abundantly above all that I can think or imagine as I trust in you. I invite you to prune my life, showing me what needs to go and what needs to stay, so that I can make room for the new you want to do in and through me. Please give me the strength and grace to obey so that I can continue to produce abundant fruit in season after season.

In Jesus' name,

Amen

Story of Flourishing:

A few years ago, my faith and obedience were tested in a way I didn't see coming. After giving birth to my beautiful son, I eagerly anticipated taking him home. However, instead, the joy of giving birth quickly cascaded into concern when his sudden health challenges put him in the NICU. As a new mother, this fractured my soul.

By the grace of God and the hands of a gracious medical staff, Josiah began recovery at home after a few days. I determined in my heart not to go back to work so that I could protect him as much as possible to ensure his continued health. I felt I needed to focus completely on him, thinking I could not possibly be a nurturing mom while working in the fast-paced environment of live television.

When I prayed, though, God challenged my thought process. After my 12-week maternity leave ended, I felt Him leading me to step back into my career in television. It was incredibly hard, but I knew I needed to surrender my will. I understood that my disobedience to God's leading wouldn't protect my son. Only the path of obedience would allow me to flourish. It was challenging, but as I obeyed, God aligned every area of my life in ways that were unmistakably marked by His favor.

The young lady who watched my son during the day ended up giving her life to Christ and embarking on a journey of freedom. Within a year, God blessed me with the desire of my heart. I spent a season at home with my kids after finishing a season in television. I found that the decision to follow His path was not about choosing to *either* be excellent as a mom or excellent in the workplace. God was equipping me for *both*. He was looking for *expansion*—not *restriction*.

Now, years later, I see how that stretching season was preparing and strengthening me for the assignment I am walking in today as a wife, mother, pastor, producer, and college professor. He calls us all to flourish in every area as we live a life of true surrender and obedience to Him.

—Emonne

Chapter Seven

WATER THE SEED

The tongue has the power of life and death, and those who love it will eat its fruit. —Proverbs 18:21

O ur family recently embarked on a month-long summer mission trip. Since traveling with three children requires extra preparation, I took great care to make sure I forgot nothing. For about three weeks into our trip, I thought I had succeeded! But then our neighbor called.

"Are you guys out of town?" He asked.

"Yes, we are." I replied. "Is something wrong?"

"Your grass is dying!" He said.

I had *totally* forgotten about the lawn! I immediately called a friend and asked her to water it, but when we returned home, it was brown and almost completely dead. The Tulsa summer heat had gotten the best of it! It reminded me of the error in the phrase, "The grass is always greener on the other side." My neighbors would tell you— that's not true at all. The grass is greener where you water it!

THE GRASS ISN'T GREENER ON THE OTHER SIDE; IT'S GREENER WHERE YOU WATER IT!

I remember looking at the houses near ours, noticing the contrast between their lawns and ours. Theirs were green and thriving because they paid attention to nourishing them. Ours was brown and dying because we didn't. For the few weeks following our return, we had to increase the amount of water we gave our grass until it grew again. It took a while, but eventually, our lawn went back to flourishing.

This reminds me of life. To continue flourishing in every season— even the rough, hot, dry ones—we must consistently water the seeds we've planted. The watering process involves two steps, and we see them clearly throughout scripture. Mark 11:24 gives us the first step. Here, Jesus says, "Therefore I tell you, whatever you ask for in prayer, believe that you have received it, and it will be yours." We have access to *all* of God's promises! Not *some* of them. *All* of them. But we have to do our part! We have to believe it.

We discussed the second part of the process in chapter three: we must also speak it. Joshua 1:8 instructs, "Keep this Book of the Law always on your lips; meditate on it day and night, so that you may be careful to do everything written in it. Then you will be prosperous and successful."

We see both steps confirmed through the story in Ezekiel 37:1-14. In this passage, God showed Ezekiel a vision of a valley of dry bones. The Lord asked, "Can these bones live?" Ezekiel responded, "Sovereign Lord, you alone know." So, in verses four through six, the Lord commanded him:

> "... Prophesy to these bones and say to them, 'Dry bones, hear the word of the Lord! This is what the Sovereign Lord says to these bones: I will make breath enter you, and you will come to life. I will attach tendons to you and make flesh come upon you and cover you with skin; I will put breath in you, and you will come to life. Then you will know that I am the Lord.'"

As Ezekiel obeyed—first believing and then prophesying—the dry bones did exactly as God said. They rattled, joined, formed skin, and received breath, forming a great army. *That's* the power of faith-filled words!

In what areas of your life do you need to believe again? To speak faith over? I can hear the Lord asking you just as He asked Ezekiel, "Can these bones live? What do you believe?" For dead things to come to life in our situations, we too have to embrace *both* parts of this process. First, we must *believe* what God says can and will happen.

Then we have to *speak* it into existence, nourishing it with the water of God's Word.

Faith in Action

I was reminded of this throughout the process of bringing our baby girl, Emma, into the world. Caleb and I dreamt of having a third child for years, but after 13 years of infertility, we had assumed it just wasn't in God's plan. Imagine our surprise when in 2020 we received the wonderful, miraculous news that I was pregnant. To say we were excited is an understatement!

Because of my age and previous surgeries, my doctor declared the pregnancy high-risk from the start. She placed me on bed rest several months ahead of my projected delivery date. Throughout those weeks, I consistently declared God's Word over both myself and Emma.

At 35 weeks, I unexpectedly went into labor. Caleb and I rushed to the hospital immediately, and as the medical staff wheeled me into the emergency room, I could see they were seriously concerned. The doctor wasted no time in cutting me open. As she did, I closed my eyes, and when I opened them, I was met with a face of shock. She threw herself into expert-action and delivered the baby via C-section, later explaining that my uterus had ripped both ways: top to bottom and left to right. Doctors still tell me what a miracle it is that both our baby, Emma, and I made it. We probably wouldn't have lived if we'd arrived at the emergency room even minutes later.

For days, I cried grateful tears! I was so thankful to God and to the doctor He graced to save our lives. Still, I knew both Emma and I had a process of recovery ahead of us. Directly after the delivery, the nurses rushed Emma into urgent care because her lungs had not yet fully developed. We contacted friends and family to pray with us, and my family and I continued to speak the Word of God over Emma. After a five-day stay, she was cleared to go home with me.

Upon returning home, I realized I still needed more time, though Emma was doing much better. As I slowly recovered, I continually claimed scriptures of restoration like 3 John 1:2, believing God for health and strength in spirit, soul, and body. God was faithful to restore these things over time. I often think about how difficult the process of bringing Emma into the world was—from the years of infertility to the year of recovery. My heart overflows with gratitude as I celebrate the fact that she is alive and healthy today!

Dodie Osteen also tells of the importance of speaking God's Word in the story of her healing. In 1981, she received a grave diagnosis: metastatic cancer of the liver, with only a few weeks to live. The doctors told her there was nothing they could do for her, so they sent her home to die. This was her *dry bones* moment. She had to believe for her healing to the point of action.

Thankfully, Dodie knew God's Word. She had spent her life planting seeds of His promises in her heart, and she recognized it was time to water them. So, she put photos of herself at her healthiest all over her house. She wanted to remind herself constantly that she *would* get to that point again. She also put healing scriptures all over her house and declared them daily. That has been over forty years now! God healed Dodie, and she has remained cancer free ever since. Jesus is the healer, and nothing is too difficult for Him! He can heal, deliver, and restore *everything* the enemy has tried to steal from your life.

In Mark 5:25-34, we find another woman with a health dilemma. She had been suffering from immense bleeding for twelve years straight. After spending all her money on doctors, she still had made no progress. One day, she found out Jesus was coming into town. She had heard that He healed people, and she believed He would heal her. So, she acted on that belief. Verse twenty-eight says that she thought, ". . . 'If I just touch his clothes, I will be healed.'" So as Jesus passed by, she pressed through. When she got close enough, she reached out and touched the hem of His garment. Immediately, the Lord's healing power flowed through her, and she was completely healed.

You may have a dream of flourishing in an area of your life, but right now, it looks dead. It looks sick. It looks barren. Choose to see the opposite! Choose to see life, health, and purpose. Then, speak it. Act on it. As you speak life over your situation, declaring God's goodness and faithfulness, like Ezekiel, like Dodie, and like this woman, you *will* see a turnaround.

SPEAKING BY FAITH MEANS WE SAY SOMETHING BEFORE WE SEE IT.

Worship in Advance

Speaking by faith means we *say* something before we *see* it. From our limited human perspective, this can be hard. When you're struggling to speak life over a situation that looks dead, worship. When we thank God in advance for what He is *going* to do, it naturally builds our faith.

God reminded me of this when our 18-year-old, Isaac, was only 3 years old. We experienced a month-long battle for his health, in which he toggled between life and death. Below is an excerpt from my book *Awake*, where I tell the story in detail.

In our family, Caleb and I have stood in faith for many things. As a mom, one of the hardest things to stand for was my son Isaac's health. During our first flight to Hong Kong, he had an allergic reaction to something and stopped breathing on the plane. He was given CPR and put on an oxygen tank. Finally, he started breathing but had another episode on the plane only a few hours later.

When we landed, we went straight to the doctor, and the next day, Isaac was admitted to the hospital. He was very weak; after the medical tests, one doctor said he might have long-term effects from this incident. Caleb and I began to pray and believe for a miracle.

The following week, we flew to Singapore. While we were there, Isaac had another episode. From Singapore, we were scheduled to fly to the Philippines. Fear tried to grip me, since I didn't know what might happen to Isaac if we traveled again. But we prayed and felt we were supposed to go.

That week, in the Philippines, I remember being in the hotel room and feeling overwhelmed by fear—both about my son's health and about our move to the mission field. In that moment, the Lord spoke to my heart: "Sing, Sarah. Worship Me." I was tired and didn't feel like singing because the enemy was trying to sow lies of fear in my heart by saying, "Why are you here? Did you really hear from God that you are supposed to be here? You need to go home and give up."

But still, in that room, all by myself, with tears streaming down my face, I began to sing. As I sang, faith rose up in my heart. My focus shifted from my situation to the greatness of God. I got the victory in my heart. Immediately, I started speaking the Word over my son with faith. I declared that he was the healed of the Lord, and that, by Jesus' stripes, he was redeemed from the curse.

This reminded me of the story in 2 Chronicles 20:3, when King Jehoshaphat was facing an attack from the people of Moab and Ammon. It says that Jehoshaphat feared only for a moment, and then immediately set himself to seek God. God spoke to him in verse 15, saying, "The battle is not yours but mine!" Jehoshaphat sent the worshippers ahead of the army and, when they began to praise God, He sent ambushes against the people of Moab and Ammon and defeated them. King Jehoshaphat faced an impossible situation; however, instead of running in fear, he sought God in faith, and God gave him direction. Worship is spiritual warfare.

During that time, as I worshiped, faith rose up in my heart, and I began to speak the Word of God over Isaac. I began to take up my sword of the Spirit and boldly declare that he was healed by the stripes of Jesus (1 Peter 2:24). I declared that he would live and not die to declare the works of the Lord. I spoke life, health, and strength over my son's body. As I asked God for wisdom, He began to show me some natural things to do to help Isaac recover quickly. As we stood in faith that week, Isaac regained strength and has never had a seizure since that day. We praise God that he is healthy and whole.

In your *dry bone* moments, how will you respond? In the seasons that the heat threatens your harvest, how will you care for your seed? I pray you water it with faith, believing God's promises to the point of action. When you grow weary, I hope you'll worship Him in advance, thanking Him for the miracle He will perform.

Friend, your words, spoken in faith, have immeasurable power. So, like Ezekiel, prophesy over your life, situation, job, marriage, family, children, and dreams. Speak God's Word, calling in favor, healing, provision, and opportunity. And when you grow tired, don't give up.

THANKSGIVING WATERS THE SEED FOR A FUTURE HARVEST.

Questions for Reflection:

1) What are some things you're believing for right now? Does your speech portray your faith, or does it work against it?

_____

_____

_____

_____

_____

_____

_____

_____

2) Think about a part of your life that seems dead. Do you believe God can breathe life back into it? If so, write out what you're believing to see.

_____

_____

_____

_____

_____

_____

_____

_____

_____

3) Now, write a declaration of faith with promises from the Word that pertain to your situation. Place it somewhere you can see it often, like on your phone or on your mirror, and speak it as often as you need to!

_____

_____

_____

_____

_____

_____

_____

_____

_____

_____

_____

_____

_____

_____

_____

_____

_____

Passage for Further Study:
Matthew 21:18-22

Call to Action:

In Appendix A at the back of the book, you'll find scriptures you can declare daily over your life. Take a couple of minutes every day to read these out loud and in faith. This one act can change your life!

_____

_____

_____

_____

_____

_____

_____

_____

_____

_____

_____

_____

_____

_____

_____

_____

_____

_____

Prayer for Today:

Lord,

Thank you for the dreams you have placed in my heart. I trust you will bring them to pass as I keep my eyes on you. Please give me the strength to stand in faith when I'm tempted to waver. Remind me to speak life-giving words when I want to speak defeat and lead me to worship when I am weary. I believe I will see the dry bones of my life come together, creating something miraculous for your glory!

In Jesus' name,

Amen

Story of Flourishing:

The Lord brought me from surviving to thriving by helping me overcome fear. For many years, I lived fearful because I didn't know the truth. It held me back from so much that the Lord had for me to do for Him and to experience in Him.

I had given my life to the Lord at 12 and faithfully served in my church throughout my teen years. Around that time, I developed a strong desire to play piano, sing, and write songs. I loved to worship and wanted to lead people into God's presence, but I couldn't imagine doing so because I was too fearful.

The change came when I attended a Bible college and started studying, memorizing, and meditating on the Word. The greatest key to experiencing my freedom was the biblical revelation of how much my Heavenly Father loves me. 1 John 4:18 says, "His perfect love drives out fear." I began focusing my thoughts on the truth of God's Word rather than on negative thoughts. It was a process to daily choose His thoughts over the lying thoughts of the enemy.

As the Word renewed my mind, I stepped out in faith and began to lead worship. This one step has led to so much freedom and joy in my life! Over the past twenty-six years, I have led worship in various settings and have served as interim worship pastor in several congregations. Renewing my mind with God's Word was key to walking in my purpose!

—Leslie

Chapter Eight
GUARD THE ENVIRONMENT

Blessed is the one who does not walk in step with the wicked ... That person is like a tree planted by streams of water, which yields its fruit in season and whose leaf does not wither ... —Psalm 1:1,3

A t both farms I visited, this truth was clear: *environment* and *input* are everything to a seed's growth. That seed can have all the potential in the world, but if it is in the wrong soil, or if it receives the wrong nourishment, it won't flourish. It's the same for us. To become all God wants us to be, we need the right *people* speaking the right *words* over us.

Scripture proves this. Throughout the Bible, we see that God's purpose for relationship is not just our enjoyment; it's also our growth— to help us walk out His purposes for our lives. Proverbs 13:20 says, "Walk with the wise and become wise, for a companion of fools suffers harm." Hebrews 10:24 says, "And let us consider how we may spur one another on toward love and good deeds." Proverbs 27:17 (NLT) says, "As iron sharpens iron, so a friend sharpens a friend."

People will either stretch you or shrink you; they will either sharpen you or dull you; they will either push you forward or keep you stuck. The company you keep and the voices you heed *will* pave the path you walk in. Show me your friends, and I'll show you your future! Psalm 1:1-3 says it this way:

> *Blessed is the one who does not walk in step with the wicked or stand in the way that sinners take or sit in the company of mockers, but whose delight is in the law of the Lord, and who meditates on his law day and night. That person is like a tree planted by streams of water, which yields its fruit in season and whose leaf does not wither—whatever they do prospers.*

SHOW ME YOUR FRIENDS, AND I'LL SHOW YOU YOUR FUTURE!

This passage reminds us of the amazing benefits of monitoring the environments of our lives. We all know there are certain things we have no say over. We have no control over our upbringing, our families, or the choices of others, but we can control the environments we regularly place ourselves in. This is crucial to our growth, because while every future with God is bright, it's up to *us* to walk into that bright future. When we consistently put ourselves in the right places, with the right people, God promises we can *flourish* in every season—no matter what opposition we face!

When God spoke to Caleb and me to move our family to the mission field, we took this principle seriously. We didn't want to trust just anyone with our dream-seed, especially in its fragile infancy. We only wanted to expose it to those we knew would provide the proper nourishment for it to grow.

GOD'S PURPOSE FOR RELATIONSHIP IS NOT JUST OUR ENJOYMENT; IT'S ALSO FOR OUR GROWTH.

The first person we told was my dad, who was also our pastor and my boss. We knew he was a man of faith and wanted the best for us, so we valued his counsel. His response nourished our seed. He agreed with our faith and encouraged us to obey God's voice. He said, "Sarah, the most important thing is that you hear and obey God, because His plans are the best plans." Then, he helped us know how to prepare well for our mission, both spiritually and practically. He also connected us with everyone he knew who could help.

In the months that followed, Caleb and I walked out the wise counsel we'd received, resolving to continue nourishing our seed on our own. I did this by reading books and listening to messages on stepping out in faith. I also talked with people who had completed projects similar to the ones we were believing to complete. Their examples fed my faith.

Still, during this season of preparation, there were times it would have been easy to give up on our seed. The dream was hard to explain and often felt much too big for us. Thank God, we didn't give up! Instead, we continually sought the right environment and input. We nourished the seed until it produced a wonderful harvest.

INPUT SHAPES OUTLOOK, AND OUTLOOK SHAPES BEHAVIOR.

What seed has God given you? Is it in an environment it can grow in? If not, make adjustments. Put yourself around people who will speak God's Word over you and the dreams He has given you. If you do, God will be faithful to exceed your expectations, causing your life to flourish in ways you never thought were possible.

A Crab in the Bucket

I've heard it said that if you want to keep one crab in a bucket, put more with it. Why? Because every time one crab tries to climb out, another pulls him down. They don't want anyone leaving their group! Some people can be this way, too. Anytime we try to rise higher, they attempt to pull us down. When we try to flourish, they tell us why we can't.

These people's comments may be fueled more by their own disappointment than by an evil heart. Still, it's vital that we recognize their effect on our lives. Input will always shape outlook, and outlook will always shape behavior. That's why Proverbs 12:26 says, "The righteous choose their friends carefully, but the way of the wicked leads them astray." We need people who will encourage us to *flourish*—not persuade us to *fall*.

One of my favorite examples of this is the relationship between Mary, Jesus' mother, and Elizabeth, her cousin. The gospels tell us that Mary had miraculously conceived a child, and she was carrying God's only son, Jesus. I'm sure she had questions. I'm certain she struggled with doubt, and I know there were times she had to have wondered what people thought about her.

During her pregnancy, as she waited on the promise God had given her, Mary had an important choice to make. What environment would she place her dream-seed in? What type of nourishment would she allow it to receive? Her choice would determine her future, as well as the futures of those who followed. Thankfully for her and for us, she chose the right one. She put herself around the right person—one who would help her seed flourish.

In Luke 1:39-45, we read that Mary traveled far to see Elizabeth. Since she was expecting, it was especially difficult for her to get there, but she knew the journey would prove worth the work. She was confident Elizabeth would speak words she needed to hear, partly because Elizabeth knew something about believing for miracles. She was carrying her own miracle inside! She had become pregnant in her old age and was now carrying John—later known as John the Baptist.

Scripture says that as soon as Elizabeth greeted Mary, the baby in Mary's womb leapt. Elizabeth then prophesied over her, speaking favor, blessing, and grace over her life and the life of her child. These are the kinds of friends we need to surround ourselves with—friends who will speak hope and faith, encouraging the dreams God has given us.

If you don't have friends like that, I encourage you: like Mary, do the work to find them. Join a church, a small group, or a serve team. Put yourself around people who have been where you want to go! Intentionally invest in those who cause the dreams God has put inside of you to leap. These people won't try to keep you in the bucket. They'll encourage you to climb higher!

Keep in mind the right environment isn't just built by right *relationships*; it's built by right *resources*, too. So make sure you're feeding your spirit with things that nourish your seed—not threaten it. Listen to podcasts, read books, and follow accounts on social media that build your faith through the Word of God in the area you want to flourish in.

If you want to flourish in your health, listen to those healthier than you. If you want to flourish in your finances, listen to those who are generous and are walking in the blessing of God. If you want to flourish in the big dreams God has given you, listen to those walking out their God-sized dreams. Whoever has your ear has your life, so be wise in who you give it to!

WHOEVER HAS YOUR EAR HAS YOUR LIFE, SO BE WISE IN WHO YOU GIVE IT TO!

Questions for Reflection:

1) Why is it so important to cut negative voices out of our lives? Conversely, why should we be intentional about surrounding ourselves with positive ones?

_____

_____

_____

_____

_____

_____

_____

_____

2) Make a list of people you believe could be a positive voice in your life. Pray about ways they can influence you (through a personal relationship, or through their books, podcasts, etc.) It is best to have a mix of both personal relationships and faith-filled resources on your list!

_____

_____

_____

_____

_____

_____

_____

3) Who is in your circle that you could be a faith-filled positive voice to? How can you do so?

_____

_____

_____

_____

_____

_____

_____

_____

_____

Passage for Further Study:

Ecclesiastes 4:9-10

Call to Action:

Take your list from number two. If there is someone on that list currently serving as a positive influence in your life, send them a message to thank them. Now, reach out to someone you would like to be a positive influence to. If you feel comfortable, reach out to several people to start a small group. Then, once you finish this study, you can lead them through it!

_____

_____

_____

_____

_____

_____

_____

_____

_____

_____

_____

_____

_____

_____

_____

_____

_____

Prayer for Today:

Lord,

Thank you for the foresight to surround myself and the dreams you've given me with faith-filled voices. Help me find people who will speak encouragement and wisdom over those dreams. Send people into my life who will help pull me up, not hold me down. At the same time, please use me to be an encouraging friend to others. Thank you in advance for working in my life!

In Jesus' name,

Amen

Story of Flourishing:

At 17, I experienced a severe allergic reaction to medication that both caused my throat to swell and made me nauseous. It proved to be a deadly mix. At one point, I passed out while vomiting. Because the vomit stuck in my swollen throat, there was no oxygen flow to my brain. I was home alone for about six hours before my mom found me. She immediately called 911. The ambulance rushed me to the hospital, though they had pronounced me dead at the scene.

The next time my mom saw me, I was covered in wires and tubes. Machines breathed for me and caused my heart to beat. A doctor pulled my mom and uncle into a private room to explain the severity of my condition. He said my lifeless body had sustained severe brain damage. There was only a twenty percent chance I would live, and if I lived, he was certain I would be a "vegetable." This news devastated my mom. She had just lost my dad two years prior and now, she was being told she had lost me, too. She wept uncontrollably.

In that moment, faith rose in my uncle's spirit. He pulled my mom out of the room and told the doctor, "Thank you, but we have heard enough." He then spoke words of life over me and words of faith to my mom. As my uncle spoke, my mom recalls God asking her clearly, "Have I or have I not given you authority?" She knew then it was time to fight. So, for three days, she prayed and spoke God's Word over me. She would allow no one in the room who spoke negative words over me or my situation.

At one point, she called our pastor and my uncle to come pray over me. My mom often recounts them both speaking life over me and then calling to my spirit, "Heather, come back!" They believed for a supernatural miracle, and that is what they received! Three days later, I awoke from the coma. I not only lived, but I have lived my life to the fullest—with absolutely *no* brain damage. Today, I am married to a wonderful man, we have a daughter who loves and serves Jesus, and we pastor an incredible church. I firmly believe I would not be alive or living my life to its fullest if it were not for those who spoke life over me when I needed it most.

—Heather

Chapter Nine
EMBRACE THE PROCESS

Then Abraham waited patiently, and he received
what God had promised.—Hebrews 6:15 (NLT)

I think we'd all agree: our culture operates at a hurried pace. We're used to getting everything instantly. We can order what we want on Amazon, and they will deliver it to our door. And if that's not fast enough? Well, then we just subscribe to Amazon Prime. We have DoorDash and drive-throughs. We use the internet and social media, which both offer all kinds of information at our fingertips.

Of course, there are positive aspects to this progress. If utilized properly, these tools can help us live more effectively, saving time, money, and energy. Often, though, they're *not* utilized properly, and they end up creating more negative effects than positive ones. They leave us distracted, in debt, and stressed. We run from one thing to the next, in a constant state of haste, expecting everything around us to move as quickly as we do.

This can create major problems for us as we're waiting on our harvest. See, God isn't always fast; in fact, most of the time, He isn't. But He *is* always on time. While we might expect a "drive-through" breakthrough and a "microwave" harvest, that's not usually how God works. His promises rarely happen instantly. Scripture likens the Kingdom of God to a seed. His way is one of progressive growth.

In chapter five, we talked about Genesis 8:22, which gives the process of seedtime and harvest. We mentioned the unnamed season between the two—time. Now, let's expand on it. Waiting can be frustrating, but there's no other way to receive our harvest. Like a farmer who has planted his seed, we've got to embrace the process of growth, trusting our harvest will come in God's perfect time.

GOD'S WAY IS ONE OF PROGRESSIVE GROWTH.

It's All About the Roots

The roots are the main reason for the "time" part of the process. They are the first part to emerge from the planted seed. They anchor the plant to the soil, and then continue to expand until they're strong enough to secure an above-ground harvest.

When my family and I were living in Hong Kong as missionaries, I came across the Chinese Bamboo Tree and learned about its intriguing growth process. After the bamboo seed is planted, nothing sprouts for the first five years. *Nothing!* Still, you must keep watering and fertilizing the seed. If you don't, it will die.

It would be difficult to keep investing time and energy into something you're not seeing fruit from. It would be tempting to think, *Well, I must have done something wrong. This tree is not going to grow!* However, if you remain consistent in caring for it, in the fifth year of its growth, the bamboo tree will sprout. It's not a normal, gradual sprout, though. It can shoot up to ninety feet tall in six weeks, and it can grow up to three feet in a mere twenty-four hours![6]

If you walked by this tree every day, you'd probably assume it grew overnight, but that's not the case. It was growing underground the whole time. For five years, it was receiving nourishment to grow strong enough to hold the harvest.

This is how it is when planting seeds of God's promises. We won't see overnight results, but we must stay focused, knowing that we're developing and strengthening our roots—a vital part of the process. There *will* be a reward, but we have to remain faithful. Sometimes, like with the Chinese bamboo tree, the larger the harvest, the stronger the roots must be. And naturally, the stronger the roots must be, the longer the waiting season!

---

6 Vishal Badiani, "Learning from the Chinese Bamboo Tree," Futurpreneur Canada, April 6, 2013, https://www.futurpreneur.ca/en/2012/chinese-bamboo-tree/.

You may think, *But Sarah! I have waited and trusted for years! I don't think the promise is coming. Maybe I did something to mess it up!* If that's you, I understand your discouragement, but I want to inspire you today to keep holding on! Your harvest *is* coming, and if you've been waiting awhile, it's probably because it's large! Galatians 6:9 (ESV) says, "And let us not grow weary of doing good, for in due season we will reap, if we do not give up."

TRUST GOD'S TIMING AND BELIEVE THE SEEDS YOU SOWED WILL BRING A HARVEST.

Don't Rush the Process

Most of us know we shouldn't give up on God's promise. But sometimes, instead of completely holding on or completely giving up, we compromise by trying to create a version of the promise on our own. We forget God knows what we need, so we rush in to "help." Unfortunately, that subpar version of the harvest always ends up being more of a burden than a blessing.

This happened to Abram and Sarai (later known as Abraham and Sarah.) In Genesis 17, we see Abram was 100 years old and Sarai was 90 years old when God promised them a son. Obviously, this seemed impossible. Even so, they planted that seed deep in their hearts, watered it, and fertilized it.

Years passed, and they saw no sign of their promise. Not even a little sprout! Sarah grew especially weary, so she tried to take matters into her own hands. In her impatience, she told Abram to sleep with her maid-servant, Hagar, so she could bear a child for them. (Crazy, I know!) Well, Abram listened (Even *crazier*, I know!), and Hagar gave birth to a son named Ishmael.

God loved Ishmael, but he was not the child He had promised. In fact, Ishmael's birth ended up making life harder on Abram and Sarai for several reasons. First, because it caused Hagar to resent them. Second, because when Isaac, their promised son, finally arrived, there was obvious conflict between the half-brothers and their mothers.

Friend, don't birth an Ishmael just because you're tired of holding on. Trust God's timing and believe the seeds you sowed *will* bring a harvest. God's word doesn't return void, so put your faith in Him! Then, keep that faith to the end. I love how Elisabeth Elliott said it: "Don't dig up in doubt what you planted in faith!"[7] Don't rush the process.

---

7 "A Quote by Elisabeth Elliot," Goodreads, accessed January 25, 2023, https://www.goodreads.com/quotes/915294-don-t-dig-up-in-doubt-what-you-planted-in-faith.

Flourish in the Storm

Now, it's important to acknowledge that just as farmers encounter storms that threaten their harvest in the waiting season, so will we. One *actual* storm my family and I endured occurred when we lived in Orlando. News of a hurricane broke out a few days prior to its arrival. Every news station urged constituents to prepare for major damage, so we did.

The storm was intense. It produced wind and rain unlike anything I had ever experienced. As my family and I huddled in our home, we prayed fervently for our protection, as well as for our friends, neighbors, and church family. At one point, I remember looking out the window at my palm tree. While most of our trees thrashed around violently, our palm tree endured the storm differently. Sure—it blew around. In fact, it bent all the way to the ground! I kept thinking the trunk would snap in two, but it never did.

Once the storm subsided, we emerged from our home to assess the damage. Thankfully, we survived with no serious destruction to us, our home, or our church. All our neighbors and friends were fine as well. We thanked God for His divine protection! As we looked over the debris, I discovered something shocking. The storm had affected every tree but the palm tree. It remained completely undamaged, looking as if nothing had happened. This fascinated me so much that I went inside and researched why.

What I learned was beyond intriguing to me. It inspired me! I found the palm tree is not just abundantly fruitful; it's also incredibly resilient. God designed it with a unique bounce-back ability so that it could outlast even the worst of storms. In good times or bad, it *never* stops flourishing!

I'm not sure what type of storms you have encountered or will encounter. What I *do* know is that amid every one of them, you *can* flourish! Romans 8:28 says, "And we know that in all things God works for the good of those who love him, who have been called according to his purpose." He is going to work *all* things for good, making even the most hurtful parts of your life beautiful. I believe this with all my heart, friends—you *will* see the goodness of God!

Several years ago one of my friends, Michelle, went through the devastating loss of one of her children. We know it's the thief who comes to steal, kill and destroy, but Jesus said He came to give us life and life more abundantly (John 10:10). In the middle of her darkest moments, she chose to look to Jesus to be her strength and He gave her supernatural peace, knowing that she would see her little girl in heaven again one day. She described God's presence showing up like an "Aurora" (meaning, the morning light, in Spanish), and it ignited a greater vision in her heart to encourage women in her community. In the midst of the storms of life, she stayed rooted in Christ and He gave her the grace to move forward in faith, joy, and purpose. After that time, not only did God bring healing to her family, but God blessed them with a baby boy. Today, they have planted seven churches, and she calls her women's ministry, "Aurora," which is bringing hope to hundreds of women in multiple cities.

Though flourishing isn't something that *should* happen in a storm, with Jesus, it *does*. See, He knew life wouldn't be perfect. He knew we would face storms, but He also knew He had already secured our victory. It's why He said in John 16:33, "I have told you these things, so that in me you may have peace. In this world you will have trouble. But take heart! I have overcome the world."

Friends: you *can* overcome! When everything around you is being shaken, you can rise in God's grace because His kingdom is unshakable. You can declare, "I did not simply *survive* that storm; I overcame and *thrived* despite it!" Then you can approach the next storm with confidence, knowing that with Jesus, you *can* bounce back.

I can tell you firsthand—God is faithful. He *will* complete the work He has started in you. In fact, He is working under the surface right now, stretching and strengthening your roots so they can hold an abundant harvest for generations to come.

Questions for Reflection:

1) Why do you think it's so difficult to trust God's timing when it doesn't align with ours?

_____

_____

_____

_____

_____

_____

_____

_____

2) Has there ever been a time that you've "jumped the gun" and made a move that wasn't a part of God's plan? What was the result?

_____

_____

_____

_____

_____

_____

_____

_____

3) What are some practical things you can do to remind yourself to hold on in hard times?

_____

_____

_____

_____

_____

_____

_____

_____

_____

_____

_____

_____

_____

_____

_____

Passage for Further Study:
Romans 8:24-25

Call to Action:

Spend time creating a playlist of worship songs that encourage your faith. When you feel discouraged and are tempted to give up, turn on that playlist. Worship, reminding yourself that God is working, and He *will* accomplish what He promised!

_____

_____

_____

_____

_____

_____

_____

_____

Prayer for Today:

Lord,

Thank you that your timing is always perfect. Help me to be patient as you bring your will to pass in my life. When I grow weary, remind me not to give up, but instead, to pause and give you glory for what is to come. I trust that you are working as I'm waiting for the fulfillment of the promise!

In Jesus' name,

Amen

Story of Flourishing:

My husband and I serve as missionaries in East Africa. We both had an immense passion for the area from the time we were young. Before we were married, my husband lived in the country of Burundi, until ongoing conflict required him to leave. While there, he felt God gave him a vision to "see a healthy church planted within walking distance of every Burundian."

After getting married, I went through some health challenges, and because of them, we discovered we needed to return to the United States to pursue medical care. For several years, we lived in the Midwest, where it felt like our dreams were paused, if not completely dead. Through this hard season, we still dreamt of planting healthy churches in areas where there weren't any.

It took five years for us to begin experiencing the harvest of those seeds that we planted. It began when we partnered with Bible school students my husband had previously taught, as well as national church leadership, to facilitate church planting training. We started with one church in Western Kenya and then another one in Burundi. Soon, we were helping the national churches in these two areas develop church planting schools, plant new churches, install water projects, and launch elementary schools on local church properties.

Quickly, people were raised up to become church planters themselves, and churches began multiplying.

After only five years of focusing on church planting multiplication, we now have 160 church plants across three countries in East Africa fully operated by local leaders. Twenty-eight of these local churches have elementary schools on their properties. In the country of Burundi alone, we are now in the third generation of church planters. I'm so grateful that, by God's grace, we embraced the process of flourishing, even when we felt like giving up. Today, thousands upon thousands of people have come to Christ and joined healthy churches as a result!

—Bailey

Chapter Ten

STEWARD THE HARVEST

*You will be enriched in every way to be generous
in every way, which through us will produce
thanksgiving to God.—2 Corinthians 9:11 (ESV)*

C ongratulations! You made it to the last chapter. I hope that in
our time together, you have gained clarity, confidence, and
courage to embrace the life-changing process of flourishing. I fully
trust that you will experience a flourishing finish! As Philippians 1:6
(MSG) says, "There has never been the slightest doubt in my mind
that the God who started this great work in you would keep at it and
bring it to a flourishing finish on the very day Christ Jesus appears."
I strongly believe that the words you have planted in your heart
will produce beautiful, plentiful fruit. Now, I want to discuss what
happens when it does. I want to talk about the fun part–the harvest!

But first, let's recap our ten keys. To flourish, we must:

1) Connect to The Source
2) Get A Vision
3) Believe in the Power of the Seed
4) Tend the Soil of our Hearts
5) Sow the Seed
6) Make Room for Pruning
7) Water the Seed
8) Guard the Environment
9) Embrace the Process
10) And finally—Steward the Harvest!

How to Steward Well

When our harvest, our promise, finally comes, there are two fundamental ways we can steward it well. First, in our speech, by glorifying God, and second, with our actions, by multiplying our harvest.

Paul showed the first in 1 Corinthians 3:6 when he wrote, "I planted the seed, Apollos watered it, but God has been making it grow." Apart from God, we can do nothing. So when we receive our harvest, we must steward it well by verbally giving Him the glory! It's only *by* Him, *through* Him, *in* Him, and *for* Him that we flourish. So, praise God for *all* He has done!

The second way to steward the harvest well is through our actions. We've got to multiply what He has given us. Matthew 25:14-30 confirms this truth in a parable. I want you to take time to read it in its entirety because I know that if you grasp hold of its message, it can change everything about your future. In the parable, Jesus said:

> . . . *Again, it will be like a man going on a journey, who called his servants and entrusted his wealth to them. To one he gave five bags of gold, to another two bags, and to another one bag, each according to his ability. Then he went on his journey. The man who had received five bags of gold went at once and put his money to work and gained five bags more. So also, the one with two bags of gold gained two more. But the man who had received one bag went off, dug a hole in the ground and hid his master's money.*
>
> *After a long time the master of those servants returned and settled accounts with them. The man who had received five bags*

of gold brought the other five. 'Master,' he said, 'you entrusted me with five bags of gold. See, I have gained five more.'

His master replied, 'Well done, good and faithful servant! You have been faithful with a few things; I will put you in charge of many things. Come and share your master's happiness!'

The man with two bags of gold also came. 'Master,' he said, 'you entrusted me with two bags of gold; see, I have gained two more.'

His master replied, 'Well done, good and faithful servant! You have been faithful with a few things; I will put you in charge of many things. Come and share your master's happiness!'

Then the man who had received one bag of gold came. 'Master,' he said, 'I knew that you are a hard man, harvesting where you have not sown and gathering where you have not scattered seed. So I was afraid and went out and hid your gold in the ground. See, here is what belongs to you.'

His master replied, 'You wicked, lazy servant! So you knew that I harvest where I have not sown and gather where I have not scattered seed? Well then, you should have put my money on deposit with the bankers, so that when I returned I would have received it back with interest.

So take the bag of gold from him and give it to the one who has ten bags. For whoever has will be given more, and they will have an abundance. Whoever does not have, even what they have will be taken from them. And throw that worthless servant outside, into the darkness, where there will be weeping and gnashing of teeth.

What a strong, telling parable! In it, Jesus makes clear His definition of faithfulness: multiplication. We are faithful when we multiply the seeds from the harvest He brings. One of the best ways we can be faithful with what God has entrusted us with is through multiplication!

MULTIPLICATION: GOD'S DEFINITION OF FAITHFULNESS.

Rivers, Not Reservoirs

When I visited Israel, I noticed two bodies of water—the Sea of Galilee and the Dead Sea. The Sea of Galilee was full of life, teeming with fishermen and boaters. The Dead Sea, on the other hand, was empty. Later, I found out why. The Sea of Galilee has the Jordan River flowing in and out of it, so it stays fresh. The Dead Sea only has water flowing in, not water flowing out. So, it's stagnant, making it completely uninhabitable.

This is a great picture of what our lives become when we hoard our harvest for ourselves. If we only receive and never give, we grow stagnant. But when we live in a continual state of giving and receiving, we stay fresh and flourishing.

God has called us all to live as rivers–not reservoirs. So, when God blesses you with wisdom or insight, share it with someone. When you receive a miracle, share your testimony. If God blesses your finances, think about how you can financially bless someone in need. As Luke 12:48 (NLT) says, ". . . When someone has been given much, much will be required in return; and when someone has been entrusted with much, even more will be required." So, prove your faithfulness by making the most of your harvest. God blesses us to be a blessing!

GOD HAS CALLED US ALL TO LIVE AS RIVERS– NOT RESERVOIRS.

It helps when we realize that what we've received is not ours, anyway. It's God's. He is simply giving us the opportunity to steward it. In Matthew 10:8, Jesus says, "Freely you have received; freely give." This cycle of generosity is one that should never stop. We should always be giving to multiply the harvest for God's Kingdom on the earth. As we give, we discover people on the other side of our obedience who need what we have. If we continue to multiply our harvest, like the faithful servant, we too will one day hear those beautiful words, "Well done, good and faithful servant!"

Questions for Reflection:

1) Which of the ten keys spoke to you the most? How have you begun (or will you begin) implementing them in your life?

_____

_____

_____

_____

_____

_____

_____

_____

2) What does the parable imply is Jesus' definition of faithfulness? Why do you think this is important to Him?

_____

_____

_____

_____

_____

_____

_____

_____

3) What areas have you seen a harvest in lately? How did you steward it? How did it multiply? How could you steward it better next time?

_____

_____

_____

_____

_____

_____

_____

_____

_____

_____

_____

_____

_____

_____

_____

Passage for Further Study:
2 Corinthians 9:8-10

Call to Action:

Think of ways you can multiply what God has entrusted you with in this season. Think of ways you can be a river of His goodness. Write them down. Another resource I recommend along this line is my husband Caleb's book, *Uncommon: Leadership Lessons from Around the World*. It will inspire you to live with faith and multiply what God has entrusted you with.

_____

_____

_____

_____

_____

_____

_____

_____

_____

_____

_____

_____

_____

_____

Prayer for Today:

Lord,

Thank you for the promise of reaping a harvest of blessing if I do not give up. Today, I pray for a supernatural increase in every area, along with the wisdom to know how to best steward this abundance of harvest. Please give me the desire to share my blessings with those who need it. Use me to show others your goodness and faithfulness.

In Jesus' name,

Amen

Story of Flourishing:

One of the most challenging times of my life was when we were rescuing potentially trafficked children at an unprecedented rate. Every time we rescued a baby, our budget increased by three hundred dollars per month to pay for all their needs. At one point, I had to sell my air conditioning unit just to buy rice for the kids!

At the same time of this financial struggle, I had to make an emergency trip to America. I spent all of my savings to get there and stayed with family-like friends while there. Over dinner one night, one of these friends asked me, "Lana, what's your million-dollar God dream?" In that moment, I simply felt the weight of feeding all our rescued kids. I thought, *A million-dollar God dream? I just need rice for my babies!* Thankfully, what came out of my mouth was much different. I said, "I need land to build my dream because it's gotten so big, I can't rent the dream anymore."

From there, he pulled the bigger dream out of my heart. I dreamt of having family-style safe homes with a father, a mother, and four to ten children each. Next, he drew out the land and mapped out eight homes. He then said, "You need half a million dollars." I knew that in my current situation, that was impossible. So that night as I crawled into bed, I cried. I said, "God, I'm doing all I know to do. I'm obeying you to rescue these children! Something's got to give."

The next morning, I woke up to the news that my friend had scheduled a meeting with businessmen that wanted to help me purchase land for the children's homes. As I sat up, the Lord spoke to my heart, "And I did it all while you were sleeping. I don't need you to figure out how you feed *my* children, how to fulfill *my* will, or how to complete *my* ministry. All I need you to do is trust and obey."

The rest is history—literally, His-story! We ended up purchasing 25 acres of land from the Thai/Burmese/Chinese mafia that was supposed to be a brothel and casino resort. We named this land The Promise Land, because of the promise that in this land, we would have no lack. I have held on to that promise every day since. As I focused on planting and waiting in faith, God brought the harvest! And now, I get to share that harvest with those who need it most.

—Lana

APPENDIX A

Prayer of Salvation

If you would like to ask Jesus to be your Lord and Savior, I invite you to pray this prayer with me:

Jesus,
Thank you for your gracious gift of salvation. Thank you for your
gift of eternal life in heaven and abundant life on earth. Today, I
confess with my mouth that you are Lord and believe in my heart
that you were crucified, buried, resurrected, and now sit at the right
hand of the Father. Today, I renounce every work of darkness and
accept you as my Savior. I'm grateful for the gift of eternity with
you and for a life on earth I could never experience without you.
In your name I pray,
Amen

Congratulations! You just made the most important decision you'll ever make. You've changed your life and eternity forever! I know this all might be new to you, and you might have questions or need help getting started on your journey. If that's the case, we would love to help. Just send us an email at info@sarahwehrli.com and let us know about your decision! We will rejoice with you and guide you in taking your next steps. Again, congratulations, and welcome to the greatest family you'll ever be part of!

APPENDIX B
Who I Am in Christ:
Declarations for Every Day

1) I am a child of God. (Romans 8:16)

2) I am forgiven. (Hebrews 8:12)

3) I am the righteousness of God in Christ. (2 Corinthians 5:21)

4) I am redeemed from the enemy's hand. (Psalm 107:2)

5) I am a new creation. Old things have passed away; new has come. (2 Corinthians 5:17)

6) I am led by God's Spirit. (Galatians 5:16-18)

7) I am strong in the Lord and in the power of His might. (Ephesians 6:10)

8) I am able to do all things through Christ who strengthens me. (Philippians 4:13)

9) I am full of faith and not moved by what I see. (2 Corinthians 4:18)

10) I am the head and not the tail, above only and not beneath. (Deuteronomy 28:13)

11) I am more than a conqueror through Him who loves me. (Romans 8:37)

12) I am an overcomer by the blood of the Lamb and the word of my testimony. (Revelation 12:11)

13) I am not afraid! I don't have a spirit of fear, but of power and love and a sound mind. (2 Timothy 1:7)

14) I am a doer of the Word. I meditate on it constantly. (James 1:22)

15) I am blessed with all spiritual blessings. (Ephesians 1:3)

APPENDIX C
Watering Your Seed:
Confessions for Every Circumstance

Peace

- » I am not anxious about anything. I pray about everything. (Philippians 4:6)
- » God keeps me in perfect peace, because I fix my mind on Him and because I trust in Him. (Isaiah 26:3)
- » Peace is my umpire. It rules my heart. (Colossians 3:15)
- » I have the mind of the Spirit—one of life and peace. (Romans 8:6)
- » He will not remove His covenant of peace from me. (Isaiah 54:10)

Comfort

- » God has turned my mourning into dancing. He has clothed me with gladness. (Psalm 30:11)
- » God is the lifter of my head. (Psalm 3:3)
- » God comforts me so I can comfort others. (2 Corinthians 1:4)
- » God is my help and my deliverer. He has given me a firm place to stand. (Psalm 40:1-2)
- » God has a great plan and a future for me. (Jeremiah 29:11)

Strength

- » God gives me rest. (Matthew 11:28)
- » God is giving me strength and increasing my power. (Isaiah 40:29)
- » God is reviving my weary soul. (Jeremiah 31:25)
- » I will not grow weary in doing good. I will reap a harvest of blessing. (Galatians 6:9)

> » I am strong in the Lord and in the power of His might. (Ephesians 6:10)

Certainty

> » I overcome fear through God's love, which has cast it out. (1 John 4:18)
> » God has not given me a spirit of fear, but of power, love, and a sound mind. (2 Timothy 1:7)
> » I am delivered from the fear of death. (Hebrews 2:14-15)
> » I have no reason to fear because the Lord is my helper. (Hebrews 13:5-6)
> » I can sleep in peace, because God makes me to live in safety. (Psalm 4:8)

Joy

> » God is the strength of my heart and my portion forever. (Psalm 73:26)
> » God's love for me will never leave, and His compassion for me will never fail. (Isaiah 54:10)
> » When my heart feels overwhelmed, God is the rock that is higher than I. (Psalm 61:2)
> » God does not bring grief, but shows unfailing love and compassion amid it. (Lamentations 3:33; 55-58)

Confidence

> » Before the foundation of the world, God chose me. (Ephesians 1:4-6)
> » I am loved, accepted, and welcomed by God. (1 John 3:1)
> » I am valuable to God. (Matthew 10:29-31)
> » I am fearfully and wonderfully made. (Psalm 139:13-14)
> » I am known intimately. God has engraved me on the palms of His hands. (Isaiah 49:16)

Contentment

- » God will never leave me or forsake me. (Deuteronomy 31:8)
- » Nothing can separate me from the love of Christ. (Romans 8:38-39)
- » I am a member of God's family. (Ephesians 2:19)
- » God shows me the path of life. His presence gives me joy. (Psalm 16:11)
- » As I draw near to God, He draws near to me. (James 4:8)

Healing

- » Jesus has already borne every illness. By His stripes, I am healed and whole. (Isaiah 53:4-5)
- » I'm full of joy, so sickness can't dominate me. (Proverbs 17:22)
- » Jesus has destroyed every work of the enemy—including every sickness and disease. (1 John 3:8)
- » When I ask for anything in the name of Jesus, including healing, He will bring it to pass. (John 14:13-14)
- » He who raised Jesus up from the dead lives in me. He gives life and brings healing to my body. (Romans 8:11)

Trust

- » I cast my cares on Jesus because He cares for me. (1 Peter 5:7)
- » God gives me peace which surpasses all human understanding. (Philippians 4:7)
- » I trust in God, and He acts on my behalf. (Psalm 37:5)
- » In all things, God is working for my good because I love Him and remain called according to His purpose. (Romans 8:28)
- » Though I experience pressure, I will not be crushed. Stress will not destroy me. (2 Corinthians 4:7-9)

Empowerment

» I have received the Spirit of wisdom and revelation in the knowledge of Jesus, the eyes of my heart enlightened, so that I know the hope of having life in Christ. (Ephesians 1:17-18)

» I have received the power of the Holy Spirit and He can do miraculous things through me. I have authority and power over the enemy in this world. (Mark 16:17-18; Luke 10:17-19)

» The Spirit of God, who is greater than the enemy in the world, lives in me. (1 John 4:4)

» I operate in all the gifts of the Holy Spirit, which are tongues and interpretation of tongues, the working of miracles, discerning of spirits, the word of faith, the word of knowledge, the word of wisdom, healings, and prophecy. (1 Corinthians 12:8-10)

» I am anointed of God for ministry. (Luke 4:18)

» I lay hands on the sick, and they recover. (Mark 16:18)

» I am strengthened with all power according to His glorious might. (Colossians 1:11)

» No weapon that is formed against me shall prosper, but every tongue that rises against me in judgment, I shall show to be in the wrong. (Isaiah 54:17)

» My God is able to do exceedingly abundantly above all that I ask or think according to the power that works in me. (Ephesians 3:20)

» I am a joint-heir with Christ. (Romans 8:17)

Blessing

» I prosper in everything I put my hand to. I have prosperity in all areas of my life—spiritually, financially, mentally, and socially. (Jeremiah 29:11)

» The favor of God surrounds me like a shield because I trust in Him. (Psalms 5:12)

» All my household are blessed in their deeds: we're blessed when we come in and when we go out. (Deuteronomy 28:6, KJV)

» God supplies all of my needs according to His riches in glory in Christ Jesus. (Philippians 4:19)

» I am a giver. It is more blessed to give than to receive. (Acts 20:35; 2 Corinthians 9:7-8)

» I give and it is given unto me, good measure, pressed down, shaken together and running over. (Luke 6:38)

Love and Forgiveness

» I do not hate or walk in unforgiveness. (John 2:11)

» I have compassion and understanding for all people (1 Peter 3:8)

» I am slow to speak, quick to hear, and slow to anger. (James 1:19)

» I choose to love and forgive just as Christ has forgiven me. (Ephesians 4:32; Colossians 3:13)

» I walk in the spirit all of the time. (Galatians 5:16)

» The love of God has been poured into my heart by the Holy Spirit. (Romans 5:5)

ABOUT THE AUTHOR

Sarah Wehrli is a dynamic speaker and author, passionate about connecting people to their unique purpose and helping them experience God authentically. She has served in multiple areas of church leadership for over 20 years, has helped pioneer a church plant and mission projects around the globe.

Besides speaking, writing, and serving the local church, Sarah has an immense passion for missions. She serves as the Executive Director of Inspire International, a mission organization that focuses on evangelizing the lost, equipping leaders, and bringing practical relief to orphans and children at risk around the world. Sarah has ministered in over 45 different countries over the past two decades, even serving with her family as a missionary in Hong Kong for a time.

Sarah has a theology degree from Oral Roberts University. She and her husband, Caleb, have three children: Isaac, Elizabeth, and Emma.

ALSO BY SARAH

Awake

Scripture says that *you* have a specific destiny only *you* can fulfill. This is why it's vital to God's Kingdom that you walk in your assignment! Sarah talks about this in *Awake*. Through stories, Scripture, and implementable action steps, she helps you to awaken to your divine assignment and rise out of anything trying to hold you down. You are alive at this point in history for a specific reason. You were born for such a time as this!

Advance

There are times we all feel stuck. Stuck in pain, bitterness, disappointment, comparison, fear, or shame. We want to move forward, but how? In *Advance*, Sarah shows us. She teaches us how to live unstuck so that we can advance in our walk with God and in our purpose. Through personal experiences, biblical principles, and practical tips, she addresses topics such as moving from comparison to confidence, fear to faith, confusion to clarity, discouragement to hope, and more.

How to Hear God's Voice

Have you ever wondered what God sounds like? Have you questioned whether you could hear Him? And if so, how would you know it was Him? In *How to Hear God's Voice*, Sarah answers these questions and more. Using Scripture, personal stories, and practical tips, she helps us understand how to hear God and pursue His leading in our lives. This devotional guide will inspire you to reflect on the concepts presented, write your next-steps and implement key truths into your life immediately.

**ALL BOOKS ARE AVAILABLE ON AMAZON
OR AT WWW.SARAHWEHRLI.COM
ALONG WITH THE MASTERCLASS VIDEO COURSES.**

Stay Connected

@sarahwehrli

@pastorsarahwehrli

@sarahwehrli

www.sarahwehrli.com

info@sarahwehrli.com

Sarah Wehrli

Request an Event

Women's Events
Conferences
Weekend services
Workshops
Online Events
Retreats
...and more

If you would like to connect with our team to discuss Sarah speaking at your service, event, conference, or gathering, email us at info@sarahwehrli.com

INSPIRE INTERNATIONAL CURRENT PROJECTS

Children's Homes

Inspire International builds quality homes for orphans and vulnerable children around the world. We help meet their physical, educational, and spiritual needs through partnerships with local missionaries, churches, and other established ministries.

Conferences and Outreaches

We conduct annual conferences and outreaches focusing on equipping leaders and empowering women to recognize their potential and value. In many village outreach projects, we partner with local ministries, providing resources to help those in need. Inspire also works with leading global ministries focusing on completing the Great Commission in our lifetime.

Water Wells

With the help of our partners, Inspire International builds family and community water wells that provide clean, reliable water in needy regions of Southeast Asia. In most places, these wells are the most reliable source of clean water the villagers have.

Education and Schools

Inspire International is dedicated to bringing the Word of God and the message of salvation to children throughout the world through education and school building projects. We accomplish this through partnerships with local missionaries, churches, and other established ministries.

Fighting Human Trafficking

We partner with organizations to help rescue women and children from predators by easing the burden of poverty and supporting ministries who are making a difference.

Church Buildings

Inspire International constructs church buildings around the world to give believers a place to worship together and to help strengthen the body of Christ.

Connect with Inspire International

🌐 www.inspireintl.com

📷 @_inspireintl

f @InspireIntlMinistry

✉ info@inspireintl.com